# Handy Reference

## Office as a whole
- Ctrl+N — Creates a new file
- Ctrl+O — Opens an existing file
- Ctrl+S — (Not Outlook) Saves the active document
- Ctrl+P — Prints the active document
- Ctrl+B — Emboldens (or removes emboldening)
- Ctrl+I — Italicises (or removes italicisation)
- Ctrl+U — Underlines (or removes underlining)
- Ctrl+F — (Not Outlook) Launches a find operation
- Ctrl+H — (Not Outlook) Launches a find-and-replace operation
- Ctrl+A — (Not Outlook) Select All command
- Ctrl+Z — Undo
- Ctrl+Y — (Not Outlook) Reverses Undo

## Word
- Ctrl+Shift+F — Activates the Font button in the Formatting toolbar
- Ctrl+Shift+P — Activates the Font Size button in the Formatting toolbar
- Ctrl+E — Centres text
- Ctrl+L — Left justifies text
- Ctrl+J — Applies full (right and left) justification to text
- Ctrl+R — Right justifies text
- Ctrl+M — Applies an indent
- Ctrl+F2 — Launches Print Preview
- F7 — Launches a spell- and grammar-check
- Shift+F7 — Launches the Thesaurus

## Excel
- Shift —
- Ctrl —
- F8 —
- F2 — Launches Edit Mode
- Shift+F3 — Launches the Paste Function dialog
- Ctrl+I — Launches the Format Cells dialog
- Ctrl+; — Inserts the current date
- Ctrl+Shift+; — Inserts the current time
- F7 — Launches a spell check

## PowerPoint
- Alt+Shift+D — Inserts the current date (via the Date and Time dialog)
- Alt+Shift+T — Inserts the current time (via the Date and Time dialog)
- Ctrl+M — Inserts a new slide (via the New Slide dialog)
- Page Up — Moves to the previous slide
- Page Down — Moves to the next slide
- F7 — Launches a spell check
- Esc — Terminates a slide show

## Outlook
- Ctrl+N — (Within any folder) Launches a new item
- Ctrl+Shift+I — Launches Inbox
- Ctrl+Shift+O — Launches Outbox
- F5 — Manually checks for new mail
- Ctrl+Shift+F — Launches a specific form of the Find dialog
- Ctrl+Shift+H — Launches the New Office Document dialog

# About the Series

**In easy steps** series is developed for time-sensitive people who want results fast. It is designed for quick, easy and effortless learning. Titles include:

| General | Microsoft Outlook | QuickBooks UK |
|---|---|---|
| Networking with Windows 98 | Microsoft Project | Quicken UK |
| Networking (with Windows 95) | Microsoft Works | Sage Instant Accounting |
| PCs | PowerPoint 2000 | Sage Line 50 |
| Shareware | PowerPoint | Sage Sterling for Windows |
| Upgrading Your PC | SmartSuite (Millennium) | **Internet** |
| Year 2000 | Word 2000 | AOL UK |
| **Operating Systems** | Word 97 | CompuServe UK |
| Linux | Word | FrontPage 2000 |
| Psion 5 | WordPerfect | FrontPage |
| Unix | Word Pro | HTML |
| Windows 98 | **Graphics and DTP** | Internet Culture |
| Windows 98 - Special Edition | AutoCAD 14 | Internet Directory UK |
| Windows 95 | AutoCAD LT | Internet Explorer 4 |
| Windows CE | CorelDRAW | Internet UK |
| Windows NT | Design and Typography | MSN UK |
| **Main Office Applications** | Illustrator | Netscape Communicator |
| Access 2000 | PageMaker | Web Page Design |
| Access | PagePlus | **Development Tools** |
| Excel 2000 | Paint Shop Pro | Java |
| Excel | Photoshop | Java Applets |
| Microsoft Office 2000 | Publisher | JavaScript |
| Microsoft Office 97 | QuarkXPress | Perl |
| Microsoft Office | **Accounting and Finance** | Visual Basic |
| Microsoft Office SBE | Microsoft Money UK | Visual C++ |

Web: http://www.computerstep.com

Tel: +44 (0)1926 817999   Fax: +44 (0)1926 817005   Email: books@computerstep.com

# MICROSOFT OFFICE 97
## in easy steps

Stephen Copestake

**In easy steps** is an imprint of Computer Step
Southfield Road . Southam
Warwickshire CV33 OFB . England

Tel: 01926 817999  Fax: 01926 817005
http://www.computerstep.com

Reprinted 1999, 1998
First published 1997
Copyright © 1997 by Computer Step

**Notice of Liability**
Every effort has been made to ensure that this book contains accurate
and current information. However, Computer Step and the author shall
not be liable for any loss or damage suffered by readers as a result of
any information contained herein.

**Trademarks**
Microsoft and Windows are registered trademarks of Microsoft
Corporation. All other trademarks are acknowledged as belonging to
their respective companies.

Printed and bound in the United Kingdom

**ISBN 1-874029-66-0**

# Contents

# 3 Excel 85

# A Common Approach

This chapter shows you how Office provides a common look, so you can get started quickly in any module. You'll learn how to create new documents and open/save existing ones (on your hard disk, and on the Internet). You'll learn how to use the Shortcut bar to save time and energy, and also how to get information you need from Office's on-line HELP system (including the Office Assistant).

## Covers

Section One

# Introduction

The Standard edition of Microsoft Office consists of four modules:

- Word – word-processor

- Excel – spreadsheet

- PowerPoint – presentation/slide show creator

- Outlook – personal/business information manager

Three at least of these programs are leaders in their respective fields. The point about Office, however, is that it integrates the four modules exceptionally well. With the exception of Outlook, which necessarily adopts a relatively individualistic approach, the modules share a common look and feel.

The illustration below shows the Word opening screen. Flagged are components which are common to PowerPoint, Outlook and Excel, too.

**There are, of course, differences between the module screens; we'll explore these in later sections.**

**Outlook – because of its very nature - is slightly different. For instance, it has only two toolbars.**

**For more information on the use of the Office Assistant, see pages 22-25.**

Title bar    Menu bar

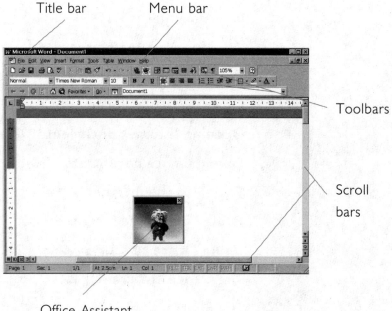

Toolbars

Scroll bars

Office Assistant

# Toolbars

**To add a new button to a toolbar (but not in Outlook), right-click over the toolbar. Click Customize. In the dialog which launches, click the Commands tab. In the Categories field, click a category (a group of associated icons). In the Commands box, drag a button onto the toolbar *in the open document*. Finally, click Close.**

Toolbars are important components in all four Office modules. A toolbar is an on-screen bar which contains shortcut buttons. These symbolise and allow easy access to often-used commands which would normally have to be invoked via one or more menus.

For example, Word's Standard toolbar lets you:

- create, open, save and print documents

- perform copy & paste and cut & paste operations

- undo editing actions

- access Word's HELP system

by simply clicking on the relevant button.

Toolbars vary to some extent from module to module. We'll be looking at these in more detail as we encounter them. For the moment, some general advice.

### Specifying which toolbars are displayed

In any Office module, pull down the View menu and click Toolbars. Now do the following:

**Outlook has only two available toolbars.**

**This is Excel's toolbar list.**
**Available toolbars in Word, PowerPoint and Excel vary slightly.**

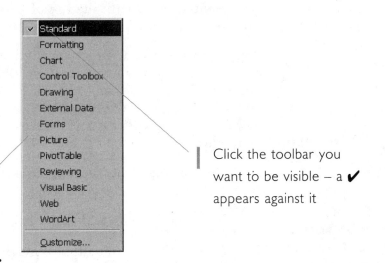

Click the toolbar you want to be visible – a ✔ appears against it

Repeat this procedure for as many toolbars as necessary.

# Creating new documents

With the exception of Outlook (see Section 5), all Office modules let you:

- create new blank documents

- create new documents based on a 'template'

- create new documents with the help of a 'Wizard'

**Because Word, PowerPoint and Excel are uniform in the way they create new documents, we'll look at this topic here rather than in the later sections, which are specific to each program. (However, see Section 4 for specialised advice on creating new slide shows.)**

Creating blank documents is the simplest route to new document creation; use this if you want to define the document components yourself from scratch. This is often not the most efficient or effective way to create new documents.

Templates – also known as boilerplates – are sample documents complete with the relevant formatting and/or text. By basing a new document on a template, you automatically have access to these.

Wizards are advanced templates which incorporate a question-and-answer system. You work through a series of dialogs, answering the appropriate questions and making the relevant choices.

Documents created with the use of templates or Wizards can easily be amended subsequently.

Both templates and Wizards are high-powered yet easy to use shortcuts to document creation. Office provides a large number of templates and Wizards. For example, Word offers Wizards which automate the production of newsletters, faxes, letters and memos, as well as numerous templates.

**The topics that relate to the New dialog, templates and Wizards do not apply to Outlook.**

All three document creation methods involve launching the New dialog. This can be accessed:

- by using the Office Shortcut bar

- from within the modified Windows 95/98 Start menu

- from within the relevant Office program

# Launching the New dialog

Utilise any of the following methods:

## Using the Shortcut bar
Within the Office Shortcut bar, do the following:

**HANDY TIP** **If the Office toolbar isn't uppermost in the Shortcut bar, right-click on the bar. Click Office in the menu that appears. (For more help with the Shortcut bar, see later topics.)**

Click here

## Using the Start menu
When Office is installed, it amends the Windows 95/98 Start menu. Carry out the following procedure:

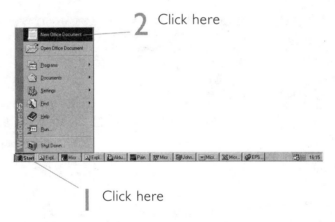

2 Click here

Click here

## From within the program
In Word, Excel or PowerPoint, pull down the File menu and do the following.

**HANDY TIP** **The following keyboard shortcut is available in Word, PowerPoint and Excel. Simply press Ctrl+N.**

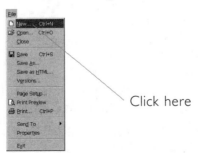

Click here

# Using the New dialog

The form the New dialog takes depends, to some extent, on which method you use to launch it. If you invoke it by using the Shortcut bar or the Start menu, you get the full version which incorporates elements from Word, Excel and PowerPoint. You can then choose which type of new document you want to create.

If, on the other hand, you launch it from within the relevant program, you get a specific, abbreviated form.

## Using the full New dialog

First launch the New dialog (see page 11 for how to do this). Then do the following:

**To create a blank document, activate the General tab and click the Blank Document (Word), Blank Workbook (Excel) or Blank Presentation (PowerPoint) icon.**

Activate the relevant tab

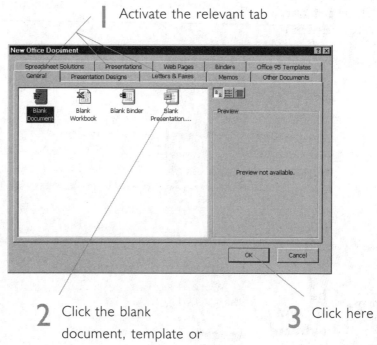

**The Preview section on the right provides an illustration of what your new document will look like (providing it's based on a template or Wizard).**

2 Click the blank document, template or Wizard you want to use

3 Click here

In the above illustration, a new blank PowerPoint presentation is being created.

## Using the program-specific New dialog

First launch the New dialog (see page 11). Then do the following:

Activate the relevant tab

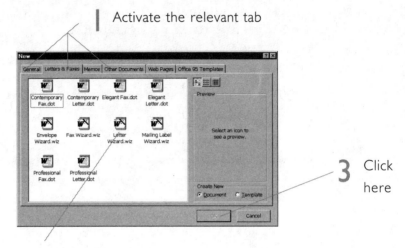

3 Click here

2 Click the blank document, template or Wizard you want to use

In the above illustration, a new Word document is being created, based on the Wizard LETTER WIZARD.WIZ.

Notice that the only new document options you can access in this form of the New dialog are Word-specific.

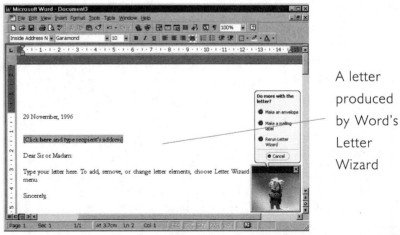

A letter produced by Word's Letter Wizard

# Working with templates

If you elected to base your new document on a template, Office creates a detailed document complete with preset text and formatting.

The illustration below shows a new Excel worksheet based on the template INVOICE.XLT.

Floating toolbar        Feature button

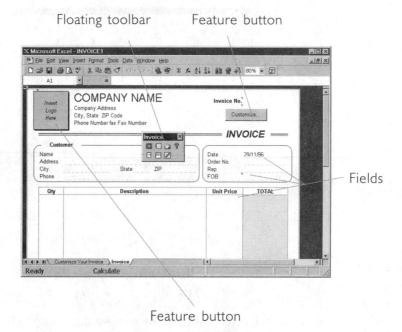

Fields

Feature button

This provides a good idea of how useful and sophisticated Office's templates are. In this case, Office has:

- created numerous pre-defined fields

- created several additional worksheets

- formatted the worksheet

- inserted special buttons which you can click to launch features directly

- launched a dedicated ('floating') toolbar

Amend these as you see fit, then save the template as a document in its own right.

# Working with Wizards

When you elect to create a new document with the help of a Wizard, Office launches a succession of dialogs. The illustration below is the first dialog when you run the Word Fax Wizard.

 **You can't use Wizards within Outlook.**

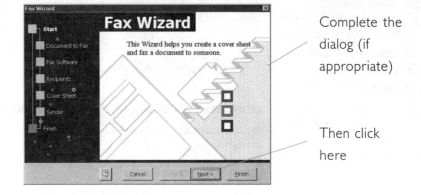

Complete the dialog (if appropriate)

Then click here

 **Office tells you when you've reached the final dialog by dimming the Next button.**

Whichever Wizard you use, in whichever Office module (apart from Outlook), complete the necessary fields and/or click the necessary options. Then click Next to move on to the next dialog. Continue doing this until you reach the final dialog. Then do the following:

 **See the 'Publishing to the Internet' topic later for how to use the Web Page Wizard in Word.**

Click here

The end result of using a Wizard is the same as using a template: a feature-rich document which you can amend as necessary.

# Opening Office documents

We saw earlier that Office lets you create new documents in various ways. You can also open Word, Excel and PowerPoint documents you've already created.

**HANDY TIP**

**For how to open an existing schedule or contact/task list in Outlook, see Section 5.**

In any module apart from Outlook, pull down the File menu and click Open.

**3** Click here. In the drop-down list, click the drive that hosts the document

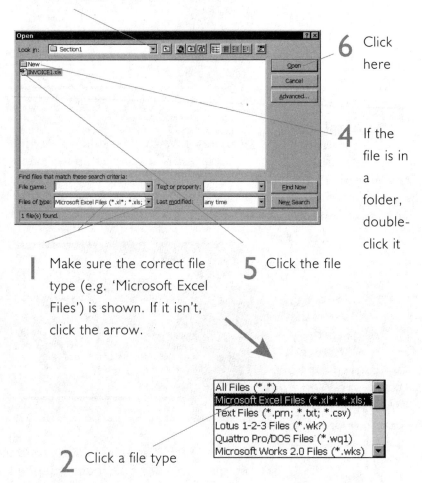

**6** Click here

**4** If the file is in a folder, double-click it

**5** Click the file

**|** Make sure the correct file type (e.g. 'Microsoft Excel Files') is shown. If it isn't, click the arrow.

All Files (*.*)
Microsoft Excel Files (*.xl*; *.xls;
Text Files (*.prn; *.txt; *.csv)
Lotus 1-2-3 Files (*.wk?)
Quattro Pro/DOS Files (*.wq1)
Microsoft Works 2.0 Files (*.wks)

**2** Click a file type

# Opening Internet documents

**To open Internet documents, you must have access to the Internet (e.g. via a service provider), and you must have installed a modem. Additionally, your connection must be open when you carry out the procedures listed here. (For more information on the Internet in general, read a companion volume: 'Internet UK in easy steps'.)**

In any of the Office modules (apart from Outlook), you can open documents stored at any HTTP site on the World Wide Web.

If the Web toolbar isn't currently on-screen, move the mouse pointer over any existing toolbar and right-click. In the menu which appears, click Web. Now do the following:

Click here

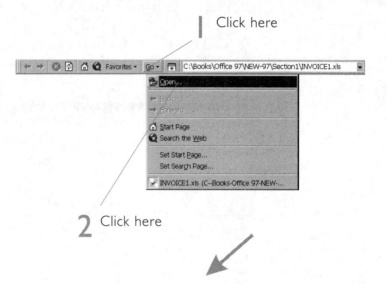

2 Click here

**If you don't know the site address, don't follow step 3. Instead, click Browse. Use the Browse dialog (a variant of the Open dialog discussed on page 16) to locate it. Click Open. Then follow step 4.**

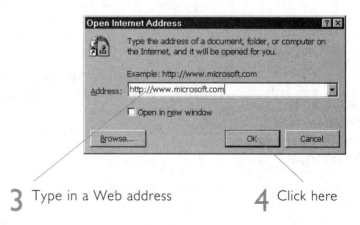

3 Type in a Web address

4 Click here

# Saving Office documents

It's important to save your work at frequent intervals, in order to avoid data loss in the event of a hardware fault or power interruption. With the exception of Outlook, Office uses a consistent approach to saving.

### Saving a document for the first time

In Word, Excel or PowerPoint, pull down the File menu and click Save. Or press Ctrl+S. Now do the following:

2 Click here. In the drop-down list, click the drive you want to host the document

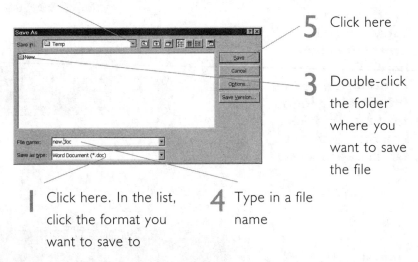

5 Click here

3 Double-click the folder where you want to save the file

1 Click here. In the list, click the format you want to save to

4 Type in a file name

**A shortcut you can use for either save method: in Word/ Excel/PowerPoint, click here:**

### Saving previously saved documents

In Word, Excel or PowerPoint, pull down the File menu and click Save. Or press Ctrl+S. No dialog launches; instead, Office saves the latest version of your document to disk, overwriting the previous version.

This is Word's Standard toolbar

# Saving to the Internet

**Re step 2 – to publish your Office documents on the Web, you must have access to the Internet (e.g. via a service provider), and you must have installed a modem. For help with step 2, consult your service provider. For more information on the Internet in general, read a companion volume: 'Internet UK in easy steps'.**

In any of the Office modules (apart from Outlook), you can save documents to any HTTP site on the World Wide Web. This is a two-stage process:

1.  saving your completed Office document in HTML (HyperText Markup Language) format

2.  copying the HTML files to your service provider

Step 2 is outside the scope of this book.

Pull down the File menu and click Save as HTML. What happens now differs from module to module.

## Word

Word launches the Save As HTML dialog. Complete this as per steps 2-5 on page 18. After step 5, Word reopens the document in HTML format. Note that some of the formatting may have disappeared or have been changed – the Web supports fewer formatting variables.

## PowerPoint and Excel

These modules launch a special Wizard (different in each). Do the following:

Complete the dialog (if appropriate)

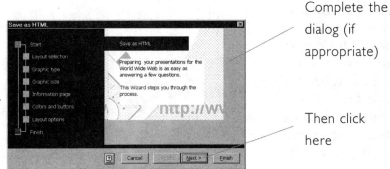

Then click here

**This is the first Wizard dialog within PowerPoint.**

Now complete the additional Wizard dialogs which appear. Finally, do the following:

Click here

# Publishing to the Internet

**To publish your completed Word document on the Web, you must have access to the Internet (e.g. via a service provider), and you must have installed a modem.**

On page 19, we discussed how to save an existing Office document in HTML format (for future transmission to the Web). However, in Word you can also use another method to produce documents on the Web. You can run the Web Page Wizard to create a *new* Web document from scratch. (After it's complete, you must still copy the relevant HTML files to your service provider – see the tip on the left.)

Pull down the File menu and click New. Now do the following:

**You can also create slide shows directly for the Web from within PowerPoint, though with the use of templates rather than a Wizard. Pull down the File menu and click New. In the New Presentation dialog, click the Presentations or Web Pages tabs. Double-click an appropriate template. Now amend the template (as appropriate) and save it, then send the completed files to your service provider.**

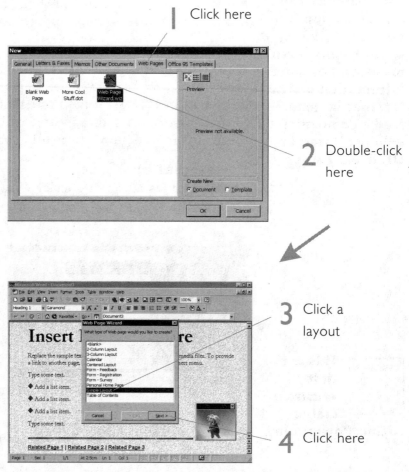

Click here

2 Double-click here

3 Click a layout

4 Click here

Now complete the next dialog, then click the Finish button.

# Using Office's HELP system

Office supports the standard Windows HELP system. For instance:

**Office calls these highly specific HELP bubbles 'ToolTips'. ToolTips are a specialised form of ScreenTips (see below).**

- Moving the mouse pointer over toolbar buttons produces an explanatory HELP bubble:

- Moving the mouse pointer over fields in dialogs, commands or screen areas and right-clicking produces a specific help box. Carry out the following procedure to activate this.

**Office calls these highly specific HELP topics 'ScreenTips'.**

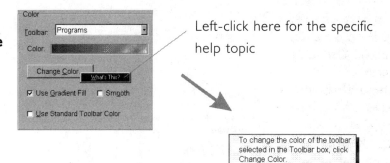

Left-click here for the specific help topic

To change the color of the toolbar selected in the Toolbar box, click Change Color.

Other standard Windows HELP features are also present; see your Windows documentation for how to use these. Additionally, all the Office applications have inbuilt HELP in the normal way...

Office also has one unique HELP feature: the Office Assistant. See the next topic.

# The Office Assistant (1)

Office 97 has a unique HELP feature, designed to make it much easier to become productive: the Office Assistant. The Assistant:

- answers questions directly. This is an especially useful feature for the reason that, normally when you invoke a program's HELP system, you know more or less the question you want to ask, or the topic on which you need information. If neither of these is true, however, Office Assistant responds to plain English questions and provides a choice of answers. For example, responses produced by entering 'What are ToolTips?' include:

    - Show or hide shortcut keys in ToolTips

    - Show or hide toolbar ScreenTips

    - Turn ScreenTips off

- provides context-sensitive tips

- offers HELP which relates to the Office module being used

**The Office Assistant is animated. It can also change shape! To do this, click the Options button:**
**In the dialog which appears, activate the Gallery tab. Click the Next button until the Assistant you want is displayed. Then click OK.**

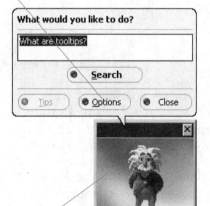

What would you like to do?

What are tooltips?

Search

Tips    Options    Close

The Word Office Assistant, after it has just launched

**If the Assistant HELP bubble isn't displayed, simply click anywhere in the Assistant.**

# The Office Assistant (2)

### Launching the Office Assistant

By default, the Office Assistant displays automatically. If it isn't currently on-screen, however, refer to the on-screen toolbar and do the following:

Click here

### Displaying tips

Ensure the Office Assistant is on-screen. Then do the following:

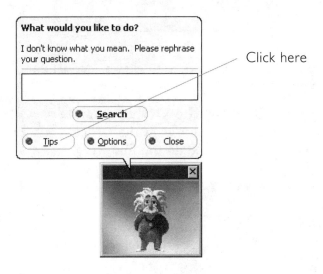

Click here

A context-sensitive tip appears. Do the following when you've finished with it:

**Click Next or Back (if available) to view another tip:**

Click here

# The Office Assistant (3)

## Spontaneous tips
Sometimes, the Office Assistant itself will indicate that it has a tip which may be useful:

 **If the Office Assistant isn't on-screen when a tip is launched, the toolbar button which launches it changes to:**

The bulb indicates

a latent tip

Click here to view a suggested tip

## Hiding the Office Assistant
If you don't want the Office Assistant to display, right-click over it and do the following:

Click here

# The Office Assistant (4)

Previously, Office had a feature called the Answer Wizard. This allowed you to enter questions in plain English. The advantage of using the Answer Wizard was that you could use it to find information on topics which you weren't sure how to classify.

The Office Assistant incorporates an improved version of the Answer Wizard.

**HANDY TIP**

**To close an Office Assistant window at any time, press Esc, or click the Close button.**

## Asking questions

First, ensure the Office Assistant is visible. Then do the following:

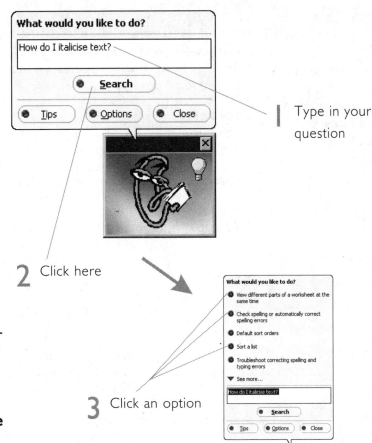

Type in your question

2 Click here

**REMEMBER**

**Re step 3 – if none of the topics are suitable, click See More. Then click the correct option in the new list.**

3 Click an option

# The Shortcut bar - an overview

As its name implies, the main function of the Windows Taskbar is to switch between already open applications. Beyond this, it has some deficits. For instance, it doesn't let you start programs directly with a single click on a button (instead, you have to use the normal Start menu route, which requires several clicks and/or mouse movements). The Office Shortcut bar rectifies this omission. You can add buttons for any programs you want, and start them very quickly and easily.

The Shortcut bar also mimics the Taskbar. If a program is already open, clicking on its button on the Shortcut bar switches to it.

**BEWARE**

**This only works with Office programs; if you try it with other programs, a second copy of the application launches.**

You can determine the Shortcut bar's on-screen location. Additionally, you can have it display permanently, or 'auto-hide' it (where it only appears on screen when you move the mouse pointer to a specific screen area, or hot spot).

## Toolbars

Buttons on the Shortcut bar are organised into specialist *toolbars*. The main toolbars are:

| | |
|---|---|
| *Office* | has buttons relating specifically to Office modules |
| *Programs* | by default, has buttons representing program folders |
| *Desktop* | has buttons representing folders on your desktop (e.g. My Computer, Inbox, My Briefcase) |
| *Accessories* | has buttons representing programs normally accessed from the Start/ Accessories menu (e.g. Notepad, WordPad, CardFile and Paint) |

You can display as many, or as few, toolbars as you want.

# Displaying Shortcut bar toolbars

Office uses a unique effect when you have more than one toolbar displayed at once on the Shortcut bar: it *layers* them.

Look at the illustration below:

Active toolbar

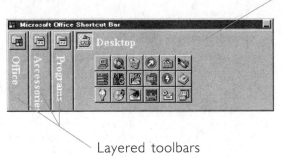

**Here, the Shortcut bar is 'floating';** for how to display it on the top, bottom, left or right of your screen, see the 'Specifying the Shortcut bar location' topic next.

Layered toolbars

To make another toolbar active, simply left-click on it.

## Hiding/revealing toolbars

Move the mouse pointer over any toolbar and right-click once. Now do the following:

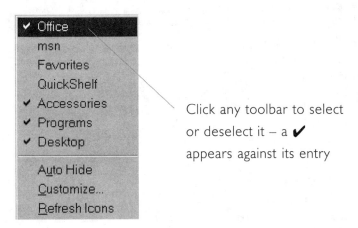

Click any toolbar to select or deselect it – a ✔ appears against its entry

Repeat this procedure for however many toolbars you want to hide or reveal.

# Specifying the Shortcut bar location

You can have the Shortcut bar display on the left or right, or on the top or bottom of your screen. Alternatively, you can have it 'float' on screen, as a separate window.

Use whichever method is most convenient for the task in hand.

To move the Shortcut bar to the top, bottom, left or right of your screen (Office calls this 'docking'), move the mouse pointer anywhere over the Shortcut bar (but not over one of the buttons). Hold down the left mouse button and drag the bar to the appropriate screen area. When you release the mouse button, the bar 'docks' automatically.

This illustration shows the Shortcut bar when positioned at the top of the screen:

**REMEMBER**

**This is another Office Assistant –** see page 22 for how to use additional **Assistants.**

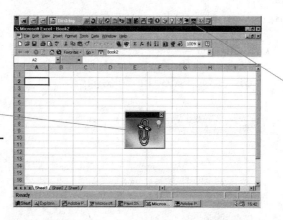

The Shortcut bar positioned horizontally, over Excel

**HANDY TIP**

**Double-click the title bar to have the Shortcut bar jump back to the last occupied position.**

Title bar

Shortcut buttons

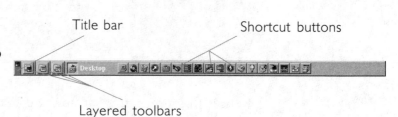

Layered toolbars

# Auto-hiding the Shortcut bar

When it's floating, the Shortcut bar behaves much like any other window. For example, if it's minimised, clicking on the Shortcut bar button on the Taskbar maximises it. (For more information on how to interact with the Shortcut bar when it's floating, see your Windows documentation.)

 **You can only auto-hide the Shortcut bar if it's docked, not if it's floating.**

If it's docked, on the other hand, the Shortcut bar can be made to conceal itself bashfully when not required. To do this, double-click in the Shortcut bar (but *not* on a button, or in the Title bar). Now do the following:

Ensure the View tab is active

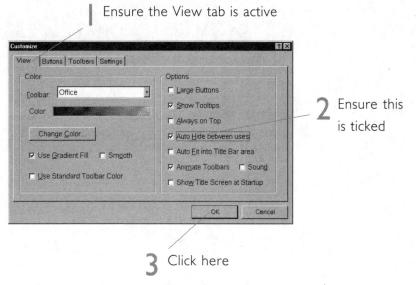

 **You can use a shortcut to auto-hide the Shortcut bar. Right-click over the bar; in the menu which appears, click Auto Hide. This procedure also revokes auto-hide, if required.**

2 Ensure this is ticked

3 Click here

## Making the Shortcut bar reappear temporarily

To make the Shortcut bar visible again when you need it, simply move the mouse pointer to the edge of the screen where the Office Shortcut Bar is docked. For instance, if the bar was docked on the bottom of the screen, move the pointer as far down as it will go.

When you've finished, move the mouse pointer away from the docking area; the Shortcut bar disappears again.

# Adding buttons to the Shortcut bar

You can add buttons that represent files to the Shortcut bar. These files can be program files, or just about any other kind of file.

Double-click in the Shortcut bar (but *not* on a button, or in the Title bar). Now do the following:

Ensure the Buttons tab is active

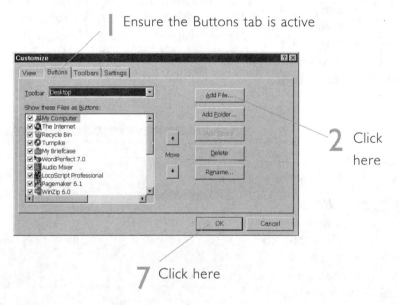

2 Click here

7 Click here

3 Click here. In the drop-down list, click the drive which hosts the file

6 Click here

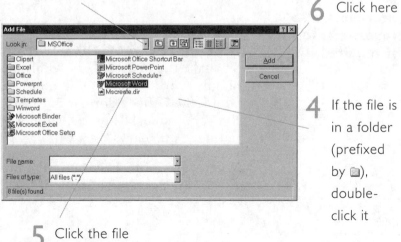

4 If the file is in a folder (prefixed by 🖿), double-click it

5 Click the file

# Word

This chapter gives you the fundamentals of using Word. You'll learn how to enter text, send e-mail and negotiate the Word screen (using the various views). You'll also discover how to format text and create/apply text styles. Finally, you'll find out how to proof your documents, create automatic summaries, insert pictures and then customise page layout and printing.

## Covers

Section Two

# The Word screen

Below is a detailed illustration of the Word screen.

**Users of the CD version of Office can find this picture – and many more – within the CLIPART folder.**

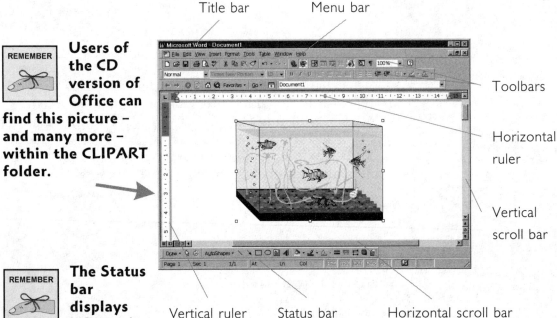

Title bar    Menu bar

Toolbars

Horizontal ruler

Vertical scroll bar

Vertical ruler    Status bar    Horizontal scroll bar

**The Status bar displays information relating to the active document (e.g. what page you're on).**

Some of these – e.g. the rulers and scroll bars – are standard to just about all programs that run under Windows. Many of them can be hidden, if required.

## Specifying which screen components display

Pull down the Tools menu and click Options. Then:

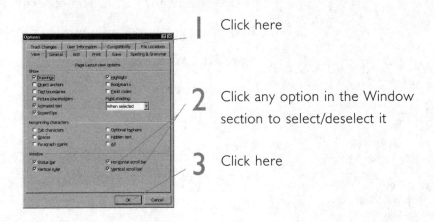

1    Click here

2    Click any option in the Window section to select/deselect it

3    Click here

# Entering text

**You can have Word insert words/ phrases for you. Place the insertion point where you want the text inserted. Pull down the Insert menu and click AutoText. In the sub-menu, click a category (e.g. Salutation) then a glossary entry (e.g. Dear Sir or Madam); Word inserts the entry into the active document.**

Word lets you enter text immediately after you've started it (you can do this because Word automatically creates a new blank document based on the default template). In Word, you enter text at the insertion point:

A magnified view of the Word text insertion point

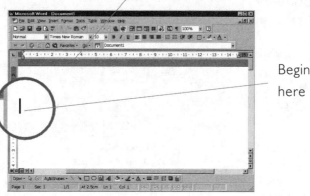

Begin entering text here

## Additional characters

Most of the text you need to enter can be typed in directly from the keyboard. However, it's sometimes necessary to enter special characters, e.g. bullets (for instance: ✍) or special symbols like ©.

Pull down the Insert menu and click Symbol. Now do the following:

**To have Word count the words in the active document, pull down the Tools menu and click Word Count. This is the result:**

**Click here to close this window.**

1 Ensure the Symbols tab is active

2 Click here; select the appropriate font from the list

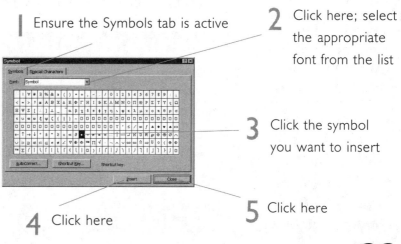

3 Click the symbol you want to insert

4 Click here

5 Click here

# Sending e-mail

You can use Word to write and send e-mail messages (provided you've also installed Outlook).

First, compose the document you want to send in the normal way. Then pull down the File menu and click Send to, Mail Recipient. At this point, Office launches Outlook in a special window. Do the following.

3 Click here

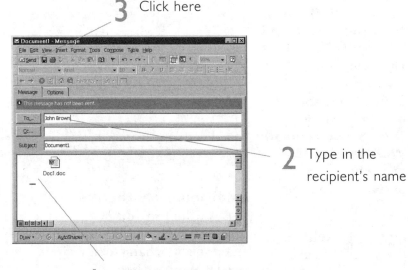

2 Type in the recipient's name

Type in a message, if required

If Outlook doesn't recognise the name you inserted in step 2, it launches the next dialog. Carry out step 4 OR 5, then 6:

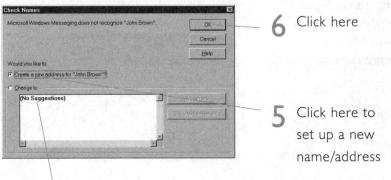

6 Click here

5 Click here to set up a new name/address

**Finally, click OK.**

4 Click a name/address you've already set up

# Moving around in documents (1)

You can use the following to move through Word documents:

- keystrokes

- the vertical/horizontal scroll bars

- the Go To dialog

## Using keystrokes

Word implements the standard Windows direction keys. Use the left, right, up and down cursor keys in the usual way. Additionally, Home, End, Page Up and Page Down work normally.

## Using the scroll bars

Use your mouse to perform any of the following actions:

**HANDY TIP** **To move to the location where you last made an amendment, press Shift+F5. You can do this as many as three times in succession.**

**HANDY TIP** **When you drag the box on the vertical scroll bar, Office displays a page indicator (magnified in the illustration) showing which page you're up to.**

Click anywhere here to jump to the left or right

Click anywhere here to jump to another location in the document

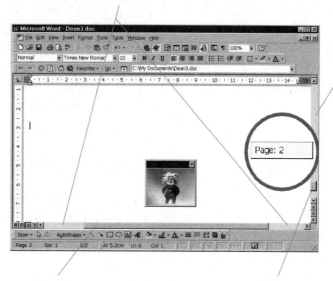

Drag this to the left or right to extend the viewing area

Drag this up or down to move through the active document

# Moving around in documents (2)

### Using the Go To dialog

You can use the Go To tab in the Find and Replace dialog to move to a variety of document locations. These include:

- pages (probably the most common)

- lines

- pictures

**You can use a keyboard shortcut to launch the Go To dialog: simply press Ctrl+G.**

Pull down the Edit menu and click Go To. Now do the following:

| Click the location type you want to go to

3 Click here

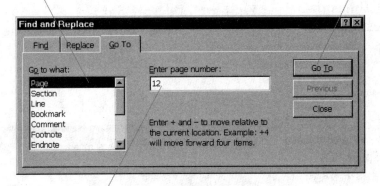

2 Type in the specific location reference (e.g. a number if you selected Page in step I)

There are some useful refinements:

- You can enter *relative* movements in step 2. For example, if you want to move seventeen pages back from the present location, type in -17. Or +5 to move five pages forward...

- To move to the next or previous instance of the specified location (i.e. without specifying a reference), omit step 2. In step 3, the Go To dialog is now slightly different; click Next or Previous, as appropriate. Click Close when you've finished.

# Using views (1)

**REMEMBER**

**There is another view which you'll use frequently: Print Preview. See later in this section for more information.**

**HANDY TIP**

**In effect, Word provides another way to view a document: you can 'summarise' it. Pull down the Tools menu and click AutoSummarize. In the dialog, click a summary type and size. Then click OK.**

**HANDY TIP**

**When Full Screen view is active, you lose access to toolbars and scroll bars. However, you can still access the menus by using the keyboard (e.g. Alt+F to launch the File menu).**

Word lets you examine your work in various ways, according to the approach you need. It calls these 'views'. There are four principal views:

## Normal

Normal View – the default – is used for basic text editing. In Normal View, text formatting elements are still visible; for instance, coloured, emboldened or italicised text displays faithfully. However, little attempt is made to show document structure or layout (for example, headers/footers and pictures are invisible). For these reasons, Normal View is quick and easy to use. It's suitable for bulk text entry and editing. Not recommended for use with graphics.

## Page Layout

Page Layout view works like Normal view, with one exception: the positioning of items on the page is reproduced accurately. Headers/footers and pictures are visible, and can be edited directly; margins display faithfully.

In Page Layout view, the screen is updated more slowly. As a result, use it when your document is nearing completion.

## Online Layout

Online Layout is a very useful view. It consists of two panes. In one, text is optimised to make it as legible as possible (the way it displays bears no relation to the way it would print); in the other, Word compiles a summary (an outline view of the document structure called the Document Map). You can click any item in the summary to jump to it automatically.

## Full Screen

Unless you have a particularly large monitor, you'll probably find that there are times when your screen is too cluttered. Full Screen view hides all screen components in one operation, thereby making more space available for editing.

Use Full Screen view when you need it, as an adjunct to Normal or Page Layout view.

# Using views (2)

**HANDY TIP**

**To switch to another view, pull down the View menu. Click Normal, Page Layout or Online Layout as appropriate (the view which is currently active has a bullet against it).**

The following illustrate the available views:

Normal view

Page Layout view

**HANDY TIP**

**Click a topic in the Document Map:**
to jump to that section of the open document.

Online Layout view

**HANDY TIP**

**To switch to Full Screen view, pull down the View menu and click Full Screen. To leave Full Screen view, press Esc.**

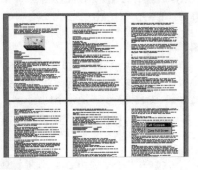

Full Screen (with Page Layout) view

# Changing zoom levels

The ability to vary the level of magnification for the active document is often useful. Sometimes, it's helpful to 'zoom out' (i.e. decrease the magnification) so that you can take an overview; at other times, you'll need to 'zoom in' (increase the magnification) to work in greater detail. Word lets you do either of these very easily.

You can do any of the following:

- choose from preset zoom levels (e.g. 100%, 75%)

- specify your own zoom percentage

- choose Many Pages, to view a specific number of pages at once

### Setting the zoom level

Pull down the View menu and click Zoom. Now carry out steps 1 & 2 or 3 & 4 (as appropriate) below. Then follow step 5.

**The Preview section on the right** provides an indication of what the selected view level looks like.

**Entries here must lie in the range 10%-500%.**

Click a preset zoom level

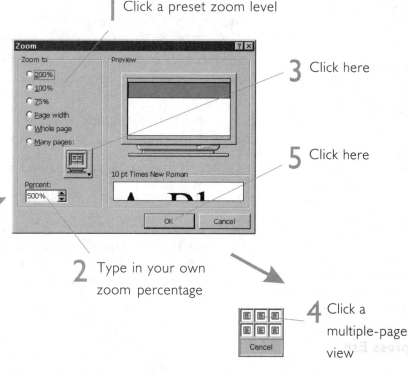

3 Click here

5 Click here

2 Type in your own zoom percentage

4 Click a multiple-page view

# Formatting text - an overview

 **HANDY TIP** **You can have Word format the active document automatically. Pull down the Tools menu and click AutoFormat. In the AutoFormat dialog, click Options. Specify the type of formatting you want applied. Click OK. Back in the AutoFormat dialog, click OK to have Word apply the formatting enhancements.**

Word lets you format text in a variety of ways. Broadly, however, text formatting can be divided into two overall categories:

## Character formatting

Character formatting is concerned with altering the *appearance* of selected text. Examples include:

- changing the font and type size

- colouring text

- changing the font style (bold, italic etc.)

- underlining text

- applying font effects (superscript, subscript, small caps etc.)

Character formatting is a misnomer in one sense: it can also be applied to specific paragraphs of text.

## Paragraph formatting

Paragraph formatting has to do with the structuring and layout of paragraphs of text. Examples include:

**HANDY TIP** **Whenever you type in Internet paths (e.g. 'http:// www.microsoft.com') AutoFormat automatically implements them as hypertext links. This means that clicking an address takes you there (if your Internet link is currently open and correctly configured).**

- specifying paragraph indents

- specifying paragraph alignment (e.g. left or right justification)

- specifying paragraph and line spacing

- imposing borders and/or fills on paragraphs

The term "paragraph formatting" is also something of a misnomer in that some of these – for instance, line-spacing – can also be applied to the whole of the active document rather than selected paragraphs.

# Changing the font or type size

Character formatting can be changed in two ways:

- from within the Font dialog

- (to a lesser extent) by using the Formatting toolbar

**HANDY TIP** **Word uses standard Windows procedures for text selection.**

## Applying a new font or type size (1)

First, select the text whose typeface and/or type size you want to amend. Pull down the Format menu and click Font. Now do the following:

Ensure the Font tab is active

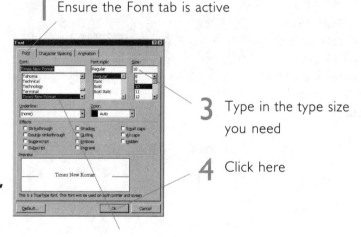

**HANDY TIP** **Re step 3 - as well as whole point sizes, you can also enter half-point increments, i.e. Word will accept 10, 10.5 or 11, but not 10.75.**

3 Type in the type size you need

4 Click here

2 Click the font you want to use

**HANDY TIP** **If the Formatting toolbar isn't currently visible, pull down the View menu and click Toolbars, Formatting.**

## Applying a new font or type size (2)

Make sure the Formatting toolbar is visible. Now select the text you want to amend and do the following:

Click here; select the font you want to use in the drop-down list

Type in the type size you need and press Enter

# Changing text colour

First, select the text you want to alter. Pull down the Format dialog and click Font. Now do the following:

Ensure the Font tab is active

**Re step 3 - clicking Auto sets the colour to black (unless you've amended the default Windows text colour).**

2 Click here

4 Click here

3 Click the colour you want to apply

## Verifying current text formatting

If you're in any doubt about what character/paragraph formatting attributes are associated with text, press Shift+F1. Now click in the text. This is the result:

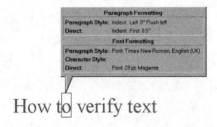

How to verify text

Press Esc to return to normal text editing.

# Changing the font style

The default font style is Regular. The additional font styles you can use depend on the typeface. For example, Times New Roman has Bold, Italic and Bold Italic. Arial Rounded MT Bold, on the other hand, merely has Bold and Bold Italic.

You can use the Font dialog or the Formatting toolbar to change font styles.

### Amending the font style (1)

First, select the text whose style you want to change. Then pull down the Format menu and click Font. Do the following:

**HANDY TIP**

**To underline text, click here:** **select an underlining type in the list.**

Ensure the Font tab is active

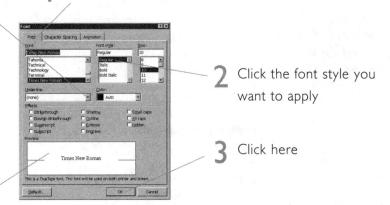

2 Click the font style you want to apply

3 Click here

**HANDY TIP**

**The Preview section provides** **an indication of what the amendments you make look like.**

### Amending the font style (2)

First, select the relevant text. Ensure the Formatting toolbar is visible. Then do the following:

**HANDY TIP**

**If the Formatting toolbar isn't** **visible, pull down the View menu and click Toolbars, Formatting.**

Click here to embolden the text

Click here to italicise it

# Font effects

The following are the principal font effects:

- *Strikethrough* – e.g. ~~font effect~~

- *Superscript* – e.g. f$^{\text{ont effect}}$

- *Subscript* – e.g. f$_{\text{ont effect}}$

- *All Caps* – e.g. FONT EFFECT

- *Small Caps* – e.g. FONT EFFECT

In addition, you can mark text as hidden, which means that it doesn't display on screen or print.

You can only apply font effects from within the Font dialog.

## Applying font effects

First, select the relevant text. Pull down the Format dialog and click Font. Then carry out the following steps:

**You can also use the following keyboard shortcuts: Ctrl++ for Superscript; Ctrl+= for Subscript; Ctrl+Shift+K for Small Caps; Ctrl+Shift+A for All Caps; Ctrl+Shift+H for Hidden.**

**Many of the font effects can be combined – e.g. Superscript with Small Caps. However, Small Caps and All Caps are mutually exclusive.**

Ensure the Font tab is active

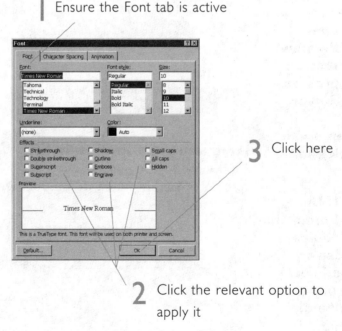

3 Click here

2 Click the relevant option to apply it

# Indenting paragraphs - an overview

**You can achieve a similar effect by using tabs. However, indents are easier to apply (and amend subsequently).**

Indents are a crucial component of document layout. For instance, in most document types indenting the first line of paragraphs (i.e. moving it inwards away from the left page margin) makes the text much more legible.

Other document types – e.g. bibliographies – can use the following:

- negative indents (where the direction of indent is towards and beyond the left margin)

- hanging indents (where the first line is unaltered, while subsequent lines are indented)

- full indents (where the entire paragraph is indented away from the left and/or the right margins)

**Don't confuse indents with page margins. Margins are the gap between the edge of the page and the text area; indents define the distance between the margins and text.**

Some of the potential indent combinations are shown in the illustration below:

> This paragraph has a full left and right indent. It's best, however, not to overdo the extent of the indent: 0.35 inches is often more than adequate.
>
> This paragraph has a first-line indent. This type of indent is suitable for most document types. It's best, however, not to overdo the extent of the indent: 0.35 inches is often more than adequate.
>
> This paragraph has a negative left indent. It's best, however, not to overdo the extent of the indent: 0.35 inches is often more than adequate.
>
> This paragraph has a hanging indent. It's best, however, not to overdo the extent of the indent: 0.35 inches is often more than adequate.

left and right indent

first-line indent

negative left indent

hanging indent

Left margin (inserted for illustration purposes)

Right margin (inserted for illustration purposes)

# Applying indents to paragraphs

Paragraphs can be indented from within the Paragraph dialog, or (to a lesser extent) by using the Formatting toolbar.

### Indenting text (1)

First, select the paragraph you want to indent. Pull down the Format menu and click Paragraph. Now follow step 1 below. If you want a left indent, carry out step 2. For a right indent, follow step 3. To achieve a first-line or hanging indent, follow steps 4 and 5. Finally, irrespective of the indent type, carry out step 6.

Ensure the Indents and Spacing tab is active

**Re steps 2 and 3 – type in minus values for negative indents.**

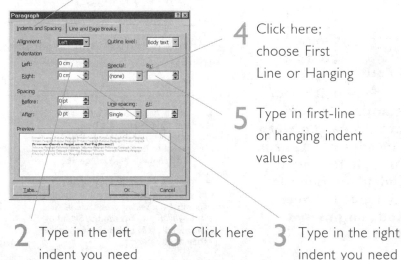

**4** Click here; choose First Line or Hanging

**5** Type in first-line or hanging indent values

**2** Type in the left indent you need

**6** Click here

**3** Type in the right indent you need

**If the Formatting toolbar isn't visible, pull down the View menu and click Toolbars, Formatting.**

### Indenting text (2)

First, select the relevant paragraph(s). Ensure the Formatting toolbar is visible. Then do the following:

'Jump' to the next tab stop

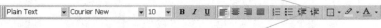

'Jump' to the previous tab stop

# Aligning paragraphs

Word supports the following types of alignment:

**You can adjust alignment from within the Paragraph dialog, or by the use of the Formatting toolbar.**

### Left alignment
Text is flush with the left page margin.

### Right alignment
Text is flush with the right page margin.

### Justification
Text is flush with the left *and* right page margins.

### Centred
Text is aligned equidistantly between the left and right page margins.

### Aligning text (1)
First, select the paragraph you want to indent. Pull down the Format menu and click Paragraph. Now:

**You can only left- or right-align text if the Left and Right Indent values are set to Nil.**

| Ensure the Indents and Spacing tab is active

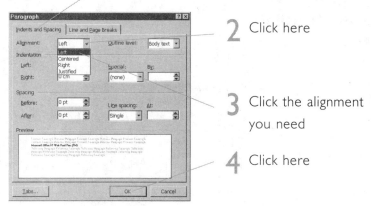

2 Click here

3 Click the alignment you need

4 Click here

**If the Formatting toolbar isn't currently visible, pull down the View menu and click Toolbars, Formatting.**

### Aligning text (2)
Select the relevant paragraph(s). Then click any of these:

Left align          Right align

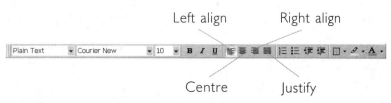

Centre          Justify

# Specifying paragraph spacing

**As a general rule, set low paragraph spacing settings: a little goes a long way.**

Word lets you customise the vertical space before and/or after specific text paragraphs. This is a useful device for increasing text legibility.

You can only set paragraph spacing from within the Paragraph dialog.

By default, Word defines paragraph spacing – like type sizes – in point sizes. However, if you want you can enter measurements in different units. To do this, apply any of the following suffixes to values you enter:

**Picas are an alternative measure in typography: one pica is almost equivalent to one-sixth inch. Picas are often used to define line length.**

- in – for inches e.g. '2 in'

- cm – for centimetres e.g. '5 cm'

- pi – for picas e.g. '14 pi'

## Applying paragraph spacing

First, select the paragraph you want to indent. Pull down the Format menu and click Paragraph. Now carry out the steps below:

Ensure the Indents and Spacing tab is active

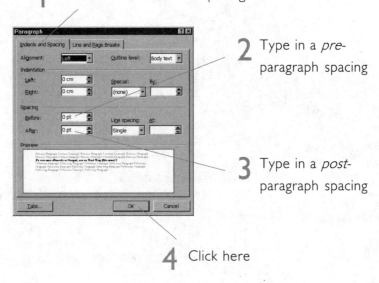

2 Type in a *pre-*paragraph spacing

3 Type in a *post-*paragraph spacing

4 Click here

# Line spacing - an overview

It's often necessary to amend line spacing. This is the vertical distance between individual lines of text, or more accurately between the baseline (the imaginary line on which text appears to sit) of one line and the baseline of the previous.

Word lets you apply a variety of line spacing settings:

### Single

Word separates each line of type by an amount which is slightly more than the type size. For example, if the text is in 12 points, the gap between lines is just over 12 points. Newspapers, particularly, use single line spacing.

This is Word's default.

### 1.5 Lines

150% of single line spacing.

### Double

200% of single line spacing. Manuscripts of all descriptions are nearly always prepared with double line spacing.

### At Least

Sets the minimum line height at the value you specify; Word can adjust the line spacing to fit the constituent character sizes.

### Exactly

Sets the value you specify as an unvarying line height: Word cannot adjust it.

### Multiple

Sets line height as a multiple of single-spaced text. For example, specifying '3.5' here initiates a line height of 3.5 lines.

**Line spacing is also known as leading (pronounced 'ledding').**

# Adjusting line spacing

First, select the relevant paragraph(s). Then move the mouse pointer over them and right-click. Do the following:

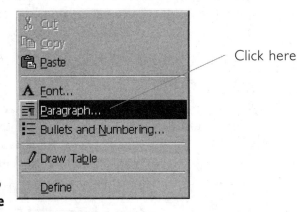

Click here

**If you've just created a new document, you can set the line spacing *before* you begin to enter text. With the insertion point at the start of the document, follow the procedures outlined here.**

Now perform step 1 below. If you want to apply a preset spacing, follow step 2. To implement your own spacing, carry out steps 3 and 4 instead. Finally, follow step 5:

| Ensure the Indents and Spacing tab is active

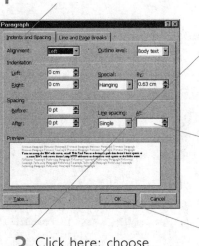

**2** Click here; choose Single, 1.5 Lines or Double in the list

**You can use these keyboard shortcuts to adjust line spacing: Ctrl+1, single spacing; Ctrl+5, 1.5 spacing; Ctrl+2, double spacing.**

**4** If you followed step 3, type in the amount of line spacing

**3** Click here; choose At Least, Exactly or Multiple in the list

**5** Click here

# Paragraph borders

By default, Word does not border paragraph text. However, you can apply a wide selection of borders if you want. You can specify:

**You can also border selected text *within* a paragraph. However, the Borders tab is then slightly different (e.g. you can't deselect the border for specific sides).**

- the type and thickness of the border

- how many sides the border should have

- the border colour

- whether the text is shadowed or in 3-D

- the distance of the border from the text

## Applying a border

First, select the paragraph(s) you want to border. Then pull down the Format menu and click Borders and Shading. Now do the following, as appropriate:

**To set the distance from the border to the enclosed text, click Options. Insert the relevant distances and click OK. Then follow step 6.**

1 Ensure the Borders tab is active

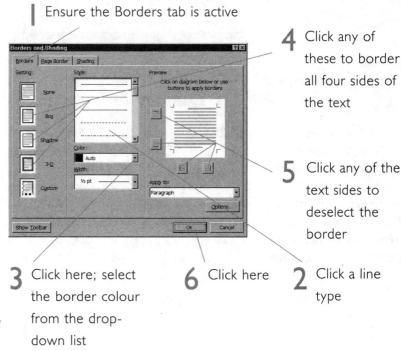

4 Click any of these to border all four sides of the text

5 Click any of the text sides to deselect the border

**Use step 5 to deselect the top, bottom, left or right paragraph borders. If you want to deselect more than one, repeat step 5 as often as necessary.**

3 Click here; select the border colour from the drop-down list

6 Click here

2 Click a line type

# Paragraph fills

By default, Word does not apply a fill to text paragraphs. However, you can do the following if you want:

- specify a percentage fill e.g. 20% (light grey) or 85% (very dark grey)

- apply a simple pattern, if required

- specify a background fill colour

- specify a pattern colour

### Applying a fill

First, select the paragraph(s) you want to fill. Then pull down the Format menu and click Borders and Shading. Now carry out step 1 below. Follow steps 2, 3 or 4 as appropriate. Finally, carry out step 5:

1 Ensure the Shading tab is active

4 Click a background fill colour

**HANDY TIP**

**Re steps 3 and 4 – you can achieve unique blends by applying different pattern and background colours. Try reversing the order of these steps, too: this varies the result.**

Borders and Shading

Borders | Page Border | Shading

Fill

None

Gray-25%

Patterns
Style:
Dk Dwn Diagonal

Color:
Auto

Preview

Apply to:
Paragraph

Show Toolbar          OK          Cancel

2 Click here; select a % fill or pattern from the list

3 Click here; select a pattern colour from the drop-down list

5 Click here

# Working with tabs

Tabs are a means of indenting the first line of text paragraphs (you can also use indents for this purpose).

When you press the Tab key while the text-insertion point is at the start of a paragraph, the text in the first line jumps to the next tab stop. This is a useful way to increase the legibility of your text. Word lets you set tab stops with great precision.

**Never use the Space Bar to indent paragraphs: spaces vary in size according to the typeface and type size applying to specific paragraphs.**

By default, Word inserts tab stops automatically every half an inch. If you want, you can enter new or revised tab stop positions individually.

## Setting tab stops

First, select the paragraph(s) in which you need to set tab stops. Pull down the Format menu and click Tabs. Now carry out step 1 below. If you want to implement a new default tab stop position, follow step 2. If you need to set up individual tab stops, carry out steps 3 AND 4 as often as necessary. Finally, follow step 5 to confirm your changes.

**When you've performed steps 3 & 4, the individual tab stop position appears here:**

2 Type in the new tab stop default (e.g. 0.35")

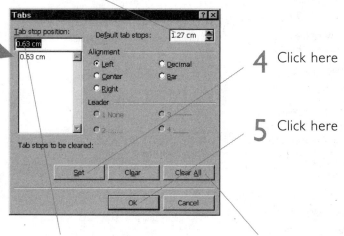

4 Click here

5 Click here

3 Type in a single tab stop position

| Click here to remove all existing tab stop positions

# Searching for text

Word lets you search for specific text within the active document. Even better, however, you can also search for character or paragraph formatting, either separately from the text search or at the same time.

For example, you can if you want have Word locate all instances of the word 'information'. Or you could have it find all italicised words, whatever they are. Similarly, you could have it flag all instances of '*information*'.

You can also:

• limit the search to words which match the case of the text you specify (e.g. if you search for 'Man', Word will not flag 'man' or 'MAN')

• limit the search to whole words (e.g. if you search for 'nation', Word will not flag 'international')

• have Word search for word forms (e.g. if you look for 'began', Word will also stop at 'begin', 'begun' and 'beginning')

• have Word search for homophones (e.g. if you look for 'there', Word will flag 'their')

**REMEMBER**

**Follow step 2 to locate specific formatting. In the extended dialog which launches, click Format. Word launches a menu; click the relevant entry. Then complete the dialog which appears in the normal way. Finally, follow step 3 to begin the search.**

## Initiating a text search

Pull down the Edit menu and click Find. Now do the following:

Type in the text you want to find

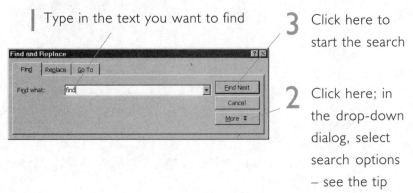

**3** Click here to start the search

**2** Click here; in the drop-down dialog, select search options – see the tip

# Replacing text

**Word replaces some words/ phrases automatically as you type (e.g. 'accross' becomes 'across'). This is called AutoCorrect. To add your own substitutions, pull down the Tools menu and click AutoCorrect. In the Replace field in the AutoCorrect dialog, insert the *incorrect* word; in the With field, type in the *correct* version. Click OK.**

When you've located text and/or formatting, you can have Word replace it automatically with the text and/or formatting of your choice.

You can customise find-and-replace operations with the same parameters as a simple Find operation. For example, you can have Word find every occurrence of '**information**' and replace it with '*information*', or even '*data*'...

## Initiating a find-and-replace operation

First pull down the Edit menu and click Replace. In the Find and Replace dialog, click More. Now follow steps 1 and 2 below. Carry out steps 3 and/or 4, as appropriate. Finally, follow either step 5 or 6:

1 Type in the text you want to find

2 Type in the replacement text

5 Click here to replace the first instance of the specified text

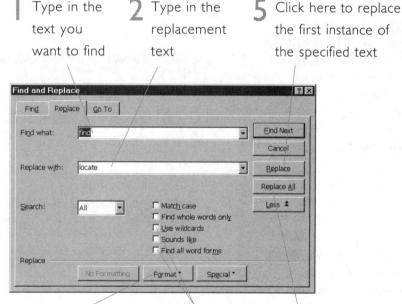

**When you follow step 3, Word launches a menu; click the relevant entry. Then complete the dialog which appears in the normal way. Finally, carry out step 5 OR 6, as appropriate.**

3 Click here to replace formatting

4 Specify the parameters you need

6 Or click here to have Word replace all instances of the specified text

# Working with headers

You can have Word print text at the top of each page within a document; these are called 'headers'. In the same way, you can have Word print text at the base of each page; these are called 'footers'. Headers and footers are printed within the top and bottom page margins, respectively.

When you create a header, Word automatically switches the active document to Page Layout view and displays the Header and Footer toolbar.

## Inserting a header

Move to the start of your document. Pull down the View menu and click Header and Footer.

**To edit an existing header, simply follow the procedures outlined here; in step 1, amend the current header text as necessary.**

**Header text can be formatted in the normal way. For instance, you can apply a new font and/or type size...**

**You can have Word insert a special code which automatically inserts the page number in the header - see step 3.**

1 Type in the Header text

4 Click here to return to normal document editing

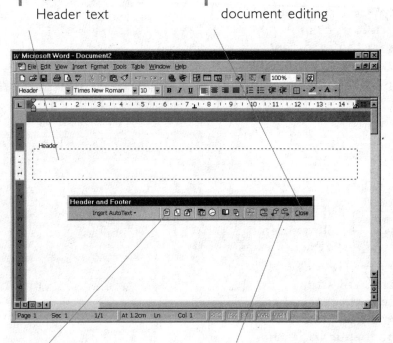

3 Click here to insert a page number code

2 (Optional) Click here to move to the header on the next page

# Working with footers

When you create a footer, Word automatically switches the active document to Page Layout view and displays the Header and Footer toolbar.

### Inserting a footer

Move to the start of your document. Pull down the View menu and click Header and Footer. Word launches the Header and Footer toolbar over the header area. To create a footer, do the following:

Click here

Word moves to the footer area. Now do the following:

**3** Click here to insert a page number code

**2** (Optional) Click here to move to the footer on the next page

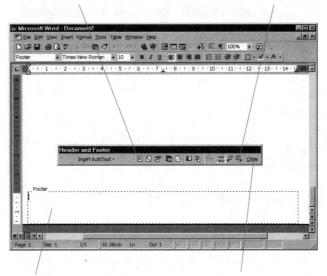

**1** Type in the footer text

**4** Click here to return to normal document editing

# Undo and redo

Word lets you reverse – 'undo' – just about any editing operation. If, subsequently, you decide that you do want to proceed with an operation that you've reversed, you can 'redo' it.

You can even undo or redo a series of operations in one go.

You can undo and redo actions in the following ways (in descending order of complexity):

- via the keyboard

- from within the Edit menu

- from within the Standard toolbar

### Using the keyboard
Simply press Ctrl+Z to undo an action, or Ctrl+Y to reinstate it.

### Using the Edit menu
Pull down the Edit menu and click Undo... or Redo... as appropriate (the ellipses denote the precise nature of the action to be reversed or reinstated).

### Using the Standard toolbar
Carry out the following actions:

**If you select an early operation in the Undo or Redo lists, all later operations are also reversed or reinstated.**

Click here to redo an action; in the drop-down list, select the relevant action(s)

Click here to undo an action; in the drop-down list, select the relevant action(s)

# Text styles - an overview

Styles are named collections of associated formatting commands.

The advantage of using styles is that you can apply more than one formatting enhancement to selected text in one go. Once a style is in place, you can change one or more elements of it and have Word apply the amendments automatically throughout the whole of the active document.

Generally, new documents you create in Word are based on the NORMAL.DOT template, and have the following pre-defined styles as a minimum:

*Normal*  used for body text

*Heading 1* used for headings

*Heading 2* used for headings

*Heading 3* used for headings

Other templates have many more preset styles.

You can easily create (and apply) your own styles.

## Finding out which text style is in force

Word provides a useful shortcut. If you're in any doubt about which style is associated with text, press Shift+F1. Now click in the text. This is the result:

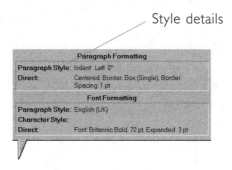

Style details

Press Esc to return to normal text editing.

# Creating a text style

The easiest way to create a style is to:

1.    apply the appropriate formatting enhancements to specific text and then select it

2.    tell Word to save this formatting as a style

First, carry out step 1 above. Then pull down the Format menu and click Style. Now do the following:

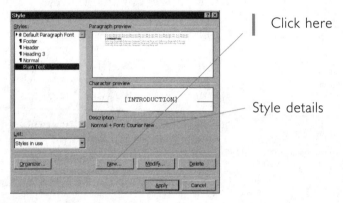

Click here

Style details

**By default, Word applies the following names to new styles: 'Style 1', 'Style 2' etc.**

2 Insert your own new style name

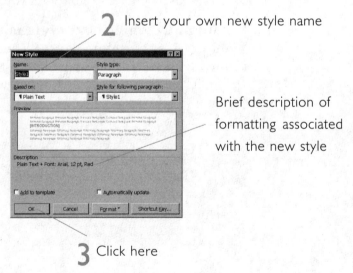

Brief description of formatting associated with the new style

3 Click here

See 'Applying a text style' for how to use your new style.

# Applying a text style

Word makes applying styles easy.

First, select the text you want to apply the style to. Or, if you only want to apply it to a single paragraph, place the insertion point inside it. Pull down the Format menu and click Style. Now do the following:

Click the style you want to apply

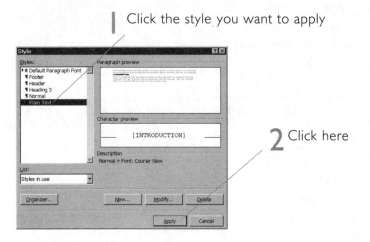

2 Click here

## Shortcut for applying styles

Word makes it even easier to apply styles if you currently have the Formatting toolbar on-screen. (If you haven't, pull down the View menu and click Toolbars, Formatting.)

**HANDY TIP** **Entries in the Style drop-down list display with accurate formatting.**

Select the text you want to apply the style to. Then do the following:

Click here

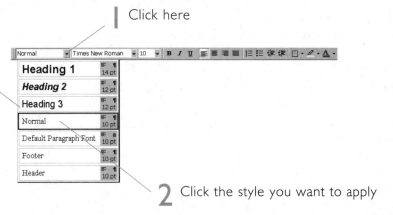

2 Click the style you want to apply

# Amending a text style

The easiest way to modify an existing style is to:

1.  apply the appropriate formatting enhancements to specific text and then select it

**HANDY TIP**

**If the Formatting toolbar isn't currently visible, pull down the View menu and click Toolbars, Formatting.**

2.  use the Formatting toolbar to tell Word to assign the selected formatting to the style

First, carry out step 1 above. Then do the following:

Click here

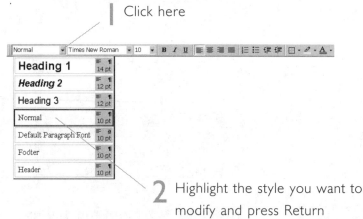

**HANDY TIP**

**You can delete styles, if necessary. Pull down the Format menu and click Style. In the Styles field in the Style dialog, highlight a style and click Delete. Click Yes.**

2 Highlight the style you want to modify and press Return

Word launches a special message. Do the following:

Make sure this is selected

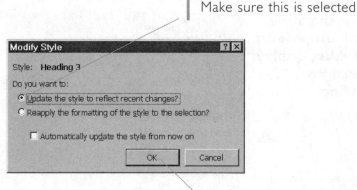

**REMEMBER**

**When you delete a style, any text associated with it automatically has the Normal style applied to it.**

2 Click here to apply the specified amendments to the style

# Spell- and grammar-checking (1)

**REMEMBER**

**Word now checks spelling and grammar simultaneously.**

**HANDY TIP**

**Word now incorporates Smart spelling. It recognizes often used names e.g. your name; personal/business names; and country names. It also detects typing patterns – for example, if you frequently type HELP Word will stop flagging it.**

**HANDY TIP**

**Here, we're correcting a grammatical error. If a spelling error has been flagged, this section of the menu shows:**

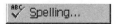

Word lets you check text in two ways:

- on-the-fly, as you type in text

- separately, after the text has been entered

## Checking text on-the-fly

This is the default. When automatic checking is in force, Word flags words it doesn't agree with a red underline (in the case of misspellings) and a green line (for grammatical errors). If the word or phrase is wrong, right-click in it. Then do one of the following:

Word often provides a list of alternative suggestions. If one is correct, click it; Word replaces the flagged word with the correct version

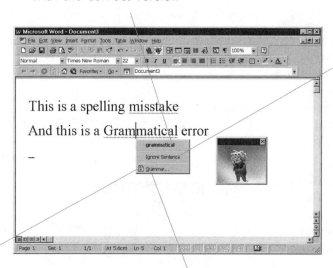

If you want the flagged word or phrase to stand, click here

If the flagged word is wrong but can't be corrected now, click here; complete the dialog which launches (see page 64)

## Disabling on-the-fly checking

Pull down the Tools menu and click Options. Activate the Spelling and Grammar tab, then click Check spelling as you type (the cross disappears) and/or Check grammar as you type. Finally, click OK.

# Spell- and grammar-checking (2)

**Word makes use of two separate dictionaries. One – CUSTOM.DIC – can be thought of as yours. When you click the Add button (see the tip below), the flagged word is stored in CUSTOM.DIC and recognised in future checking sessions.**

## Checking text separately

To check all the text within the active document in one go, pull down the Tools menu and click Spelling and Grammar. Word starts spell- and grammar-checking the document from the beginning. When it encounters a word or phrase it doesn't recognise, Word flags it and produces a special dialog (see below). Usually, it provides alternative suggestions; if one of these is correct, you can opt to have it replace the flagged word. You can do this singly (i.e. just this instance is replaced) or globally (where all future instances – within the current checking session – are replaced).

Alternatively, you can have Word ignore *this* instance of the flagged word, ignore *all* future instances of the word or add the word to CUSTOM.DIC (see the tips). After this, Word resumes checking.

HANDY TIP

**If you're correcting a spelling error, you have two further options. Click Add to have the flagged word stored in CUSTOM.DIC (see above). Or click Change All to have Word substitute its suggestion for *all* future instances of the flagged word.**

Carry out step 1 below, then follow step 2. Alternatively, carry out step 3 or 4.

1 | If one of the suggestions here is correct, click it, then follow step 2

3 Click here to ignore just this instance

4 Click here to ignore all future instances

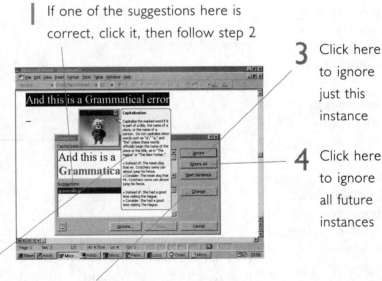

2 Click here to replace this instance

REMEMBER

**Word's Office Assistant explains grammatical points here.**

# Searching for synonyms

Word lets you search for synonyms while you're editing the active document. You do this by calling up Word's resident thesaurus. The thesaurus categorises words into meanings, and each meaning is allocated various synonyms from which you can choose.

As a bonus, the thesaurus also supplies related words, and antonyms. For example, if you look up 'error' in the thesaurus, Word lists 'err' under the heading 'Related Words'.

### Using the thesaurus
First, select the word for which you require a synonym or antonym (or simply position the insertion point within it). Pull down the Tools menu and click Language, Thesaurus. Now do the following:

The selected word appears here

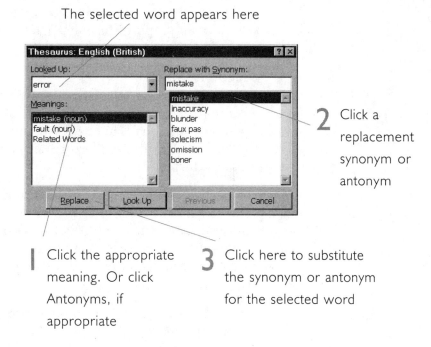

2 Click a replacement synonym or antonym

1 Click the appropriate meaning. Or click Antonyms, if appropriate

3 Click here to substitute the synonym or antonym for the selected word

# Working with pictures

Word lets you add colour or greyscale pictures to the active document. Pictures – also called graphics – include:

- drawings produced in other programs

- clip art

- scanned photographs

Pictures are stored in various third-party formats. These formats are organised into two basic types:

## Bitmap images

Bitmaps consist of pixels (dots) arranged in such a way that they form a graphic image. Because of the very nature of bitmaps, the question of 'resolution' – the sharpness of an image expressed in dpi (dots per inch) – is very important. Bitmaps look best if they're displayed at their correct resolution. Word can manipulate a wide variety of third-party bitmap graphics formats. These include: PCX, TIF, TGA and GIF.

## Vector images

You can also insert vector graphics files into Word documents. Vector images consist of and are defined by algebraic equations. They're less complex than bitmaps: they contain less detail. Vector files can also include bitmap information.

Irrespective of the format type, Word can incorporate pictures with the help of special 'filters'. These are special mini-programs whose job it is to translate third-party formats into a form which Word can use. However, several supported formats do not require filters. The two main ones are:

- Windows Bitmap. A popular bitmap format. File suffix: BMP

- Windows Metafile. A frequently used vector format. Used for information exchange between just about all Windows programs. File suffix: WMF

# Brief notes on picture formats

Graphics formats Word will accept include the following (the column on the left shows the relevant file suffix):

CGM      Computer Graphics Metafile. A vector format frequently used in the past, especially as a medium for clip-art transmission. Less often used nowadays.

EPS      Encapsulated PostScript. Perhaps the most widely used PostScript format. PostScript combines vector *and* bitmap data very successfully. Incorporates a low-resolution bitmap 'header' for preview purposes.

GIF      Graphics Interchange Format. Developed for the on-line transmission of graphics data over the Internet. Just about any Windows program – and a lot more besides – will read GIF. Disadvantage: it can't handle more than 256 colours. Compression is supported.

PCD      (Kodak) PhotoCD. Used primarily to store photographs on CD.

PCX      An old standby. Originated with PC Paintbrush, a paint program. Used for years to transfer graphics data between Windows applications.

TGA      Targa. A high-end format, and also a bridge with so-called low-end computers (e.g. Amiga and Atari). Often used in PC and Mac paint and ray-tracing programs because of its high-resolution colour fidelity.

TIFF      Tagged Image File Format. Suffix: TIF. If anything, even more widely used than PCX, across a whole range of platforms and applications.

# Inserting pictures

First, position the insertion point at the location within the active document where you want to insert the picture. Pull down the Insert menu and do the following:

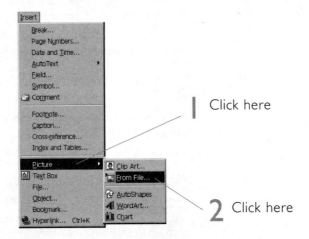

1 Click here

2 Click here

Now carry out the following steps:

4 Click here. In the drop-down list, click the drive/folder that hosts the picture

6 Click here

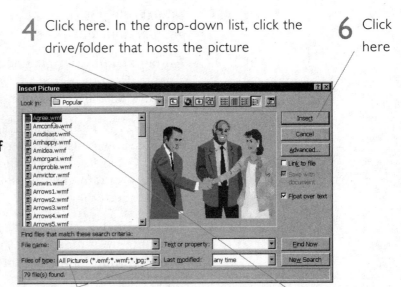

REMEMBER

**Word provides a preview of what the picture will look like when it's been imported. See the Preview box on the right of the dialog.**

3 Make sure All Pictures is shown. If it isn't, click the arrow and select it from the drop-down list

5 Click the picture file

# Editing pictures

Once you've inserted pictures into a Word document, you can amend them in a variety of ways. For instance, you can:

- rescale them

- apply a border

- crop them

- move them

To carry out any of these operations, you have to select the relevant picture first. To do this, simply position the mouse pointer over the image and left-click once. Word surrounds the image with eight handles. These are positioned at the four corners, and midway on each side. The illustration below demonstrates these:

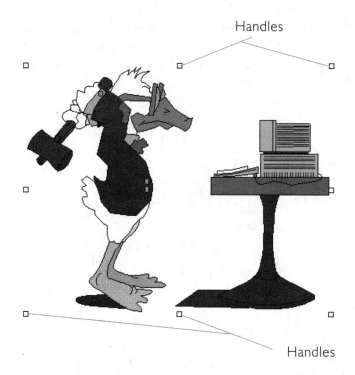

Handles

Handles

# Rescaling pictures

**To move a picture on the page, select it. Then move the mouse pointer over the picture. Click and hold down the left mouse button; drag the image to a new location. Release the mouse button to confirm the move.**

There are two ways in which you can rescale pictures:

- proportionally, where the height/width ratio remains constant

- disproportionately, where the height/width ratio is disrupted (this is sometimes called 'warping' or 'skewing')

To rescale a picture, first select it. Then move the mouse pointer over:

- one of the corner handles, if you want to rescale the image proportionately,

or

- one of the handles in the middle of the sides, if you want to warp it

In either eventuality, the mouse pointer changes to a double-headed arrow. Click and hold down the left mouse button. Drag outwards to increase the image size or inwards to decrease it. Release the mouse button to confirm the change.

**To control how text aligns around a picture, select it. Pull down the Format menu and click Picture. In the Format Picture dialog, activate the Wrapping tab. Now select a text wrap option e.g.:**

**where text aligns around the top and bottom of the image, but not the sides. Finally, click OK.**

Here, the image has been skewed from the right inwards

# Bordering pictures

By default, Word does not apply a border to inserted pictures. However, you can apply a wide selection of borders if you want. You can specify:

* the style and/or thickness of the border

* the border colour

* whether the border is dashed

## Applying a border

First, select the picture you want to border. Then pull down the Format menu and click Borders and Shading. Now carry out step 1 below. Perform 2-5, as appropriate. Finally, carry out step 6:

1 | Ensure the Colors and Lines tab is active

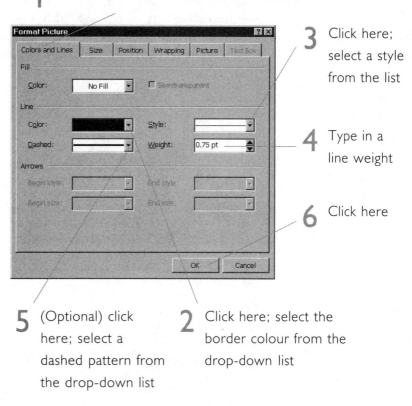

3 Click here; select a style from the list

4 Type in a line weight

6 Click here

5 (Optional) click here; select a dashed pattern from the drop-down list

2 Click here; select the border colour from the drop-down list

# Cropping pictures

Cropping is the process of trimming the edges off a picture, either to make it fit within a smaller space or to remove parts that are unwanted.

### Cropping a picture

First, select the picture you want to crop. Then refer to the Picture toolbar. (If it isn't visible, pull down the View menu and click Toolbars, Picture). Do the following:

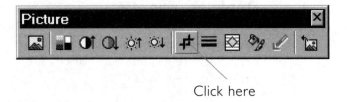

Click here

Now select the picture you want to crop. Move the mouse pointer over one of the available eight handles. Hold down the left mouse button and drag the handle inwards. Release the button to confirm the cropping operation.

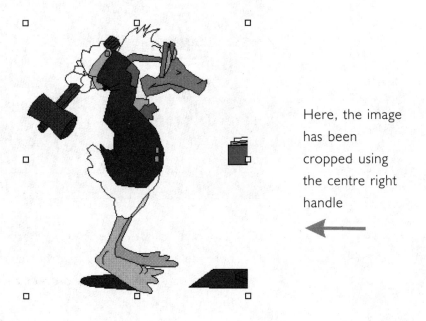

Here, the image has been cropped using the centre right handle

# Page setup - an overview

You can control page layout to a great extent in Word. You can specify:

- the top, bottom, left and/or right page margins

- the distance between the top page edge and the top edge of the header

- the distance between the bottom page edge and bottom edge of the footer

The illustration below shows these page components:

Top margin (including header)

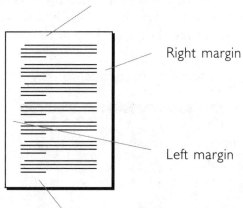

Right margin

Left margin

Bottom margin (including footer)

You can also specify:

- the page size (irrespective of margins and headers/footers)

- the page orientation ('landscape' or 'portrait')

If none of the supplied page sizes is suitable, you can even customise your own.

# Specifying margins

**Margin settings are the framework on which indents and tabs are based.**

All documents have margins, because printing on the whole of a sheet is both unsightly and – in the case of many printers, since the mechanism has to grip the page – impossible. Documents need a certain amount of 'white space' (the unprinted portion of the page) to balance the areas which contain text and graphics. Without this, they can't be visually effective. As a result, it's important to set margins correctly.

## Customising margins

First, position the insertion point at the location within the active document from which you want the new margin(s) to apply. Alternatively, select the relevant portion of your document. Then pull down the File menu and click Page Setup. Now carry out step 1 below. Then follow steps 2-5, as appropriate. Finally, carry out step 6.

1 Ensure the Margins tab is active

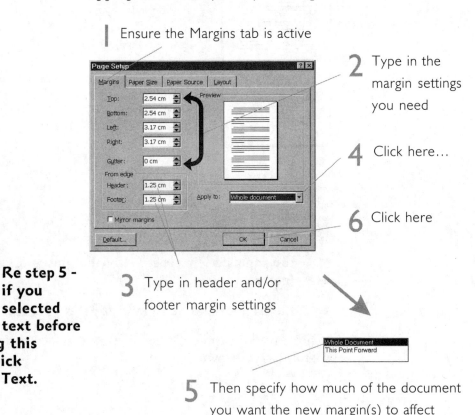

2 Type in the margin settings you need

4 Click here...

6 Click here

3 Type in header and/or footer margin settings

5 Then specify how much of the document you want the new margin(s) to affect

**Re step 5 - if you selected text before launching this dialog, click Selected Text.**

# Specifying the page size

Word comes with some 17 preset page sizes – for instance, A4, A5 and Letter. These are suitable for most purposes. However, you can also set up your own page definition if you need to.

There are two aspects to every page size: a vertical measurement, and a horizontal measurement. These can be varied according to orientation. There are two possible orientations:

**Whatever the page size, you can have both portrait and landscape pages in the same document.**

Portrait                    Landscape

**To create your own page size, click Custom size in step 2. Then type in the desired measurements in the Width & Height fields. Finally, carry out step 4.**

## Setting the page size

First, position the insertion point at the location within the active document from which you want the new page size to apply. Then pull down the File menu and click Page Setup. Now do the following:

1 Ensure the Paper Size tab is active

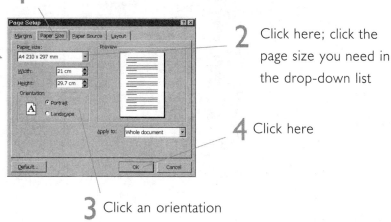

2 Click here; click the page size you need in the drop-down list

4 Click here

3 Click an orientation

# Using Print Preview

Word provides a special view mode called Print Preview. This displays the active document exactly as it will look when printed. Use Print Preview as a final check just before you print your document.

You can customise the way Print Preview displays your document in various ways. For example, you can:

- zoom in or out on the active page

- specify how many pages display

- hide almost everything on screen apart from the document

### Launching Print Preview

Pull down the File menu and click Print Preview. This is the result:

**To leave Print Preview mode and return to Normal, Online Layout or Page Layout view, simply press Esc.**

Print Preview toolbar

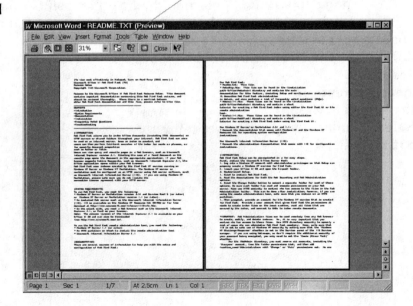

# Zooming in or out in Print Preview

There are two ways in which you can change the display magnification in Print Preview mode.

### Using the mouse
To magnify *part* of the active document, click the Magnifier button in the Print Preview toolbar.

Click here

The mouse pointer changes to a magnifying glass. Position this over the portion of the active document that you want to expand. Left-click once.

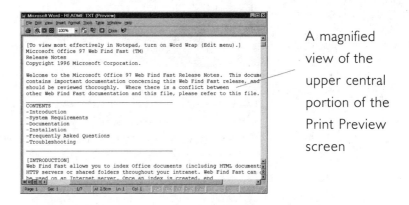

A magnified view of the upper central portion of the Print Preview screen

### Using the Zoom Control button
To choose from pre-defined Zoom sizes, do the following:

Click here

2 Click here

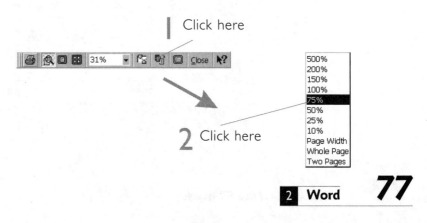

# Multiple pages in Print Preview

In Print Preview mode, you can view as many as eighteen pages at the same time.

Turn to the Print Preview toolbar and do the following:

Click here

**Word tells you here what page permutation you've chosen, e.g. '1 x 2' (2 pages displayed at full size), or '2 x 1' (2 pages displayed as thumbnails).**

Word launches a graphical list:

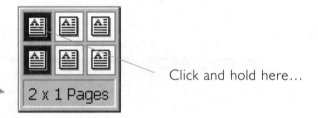

Click and hold here...

Position the mouse pointer over the first icon (see the illustration above). Hold down the left mouse button. Drag the pointer to the right and/or down (the list expands as you do so). When you find the right page multiple, release the mouse button.

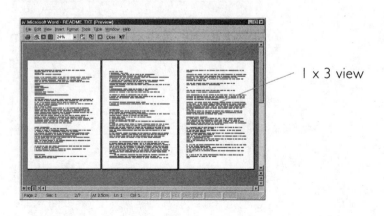

1 x 3 view

# Clearing the screen in Print Preview

We saw earlier that it's possible to hide superfluous screen components in Normal, Online Layout and Page Layout views. You can also do this in Print Preview mode. Word calls this Full Screen view.

The advantage is that using Full Screen view in Print Preview mode makes more space available for display purposes. This is highly desirable unless you have a particularly large monitor. In Print Preview mode, Full Screen view hides all screen components with the exception of the Print Preview toolbar, the horizontal/vertical rulers and the dedicated Full Screen toolbar.

### Implementing Full Screen view
Refer to the Print Screen toolbar and do the following:

Click here

**There is a keyboard shortcut you can use to leave Full Screen view: simply press Esc. Alternatively, click the Full Screen toolbar:**

To leave Full Screen view, repeat this procedure.

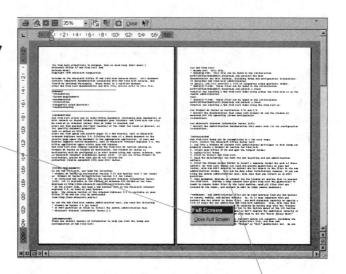

1 x 2 pages in Full Screen view

# Printer setup

Most Word documents need to be printed eventually. Before you can begin printing, however, you need to ensure that:

 **The question of which printer you select affects how the document displays in Print Preview mode.**

- the correct printer is selected (if you have more than one installed)

- the correct printer settings are in force

Word calls these collectively the 'printer setup'.

Irrespective of the printer selected, the settings vary in accordance with the job in hand. For example, most printer drivers (the software which 'drives' the printer) allow you to specify whether or not you want pictures printed. Additionally, they often allow you to specify the resolution or print quality of the output...

## Selecting the printer and/or settings

At any time before you're ready to print a document, pull down the File menu and click Print. Now do the following:

Click here; select the printer you want from the list

 **This procedure can also be followed from within Print Preview mode.**

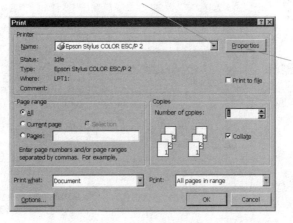

2 Click here to adjust the printer settings (for how to do this, see your printer's manual)

Now complete the remainder of the Print dialog, prior to printing your document (see pages 83-84).

# Printing - an overview

Once the active document is how you want it (and you've customised the printer setup appropriately), you'll probably need to print it out. Word makes this process easy and straightforward. It lets you set a variety of options before you do so.

Alternatively, you can simply opt to print your document with the default options in force (Word provides a 'fast track' approach to this).

Available print options include:

- the number of copies you want printed

- whether you want the copies 'collated'. This is the process whereby Word prints one full copy at a time. For instance, if you're printing three copies of a 40-page document, Word prints pages 1-40 of the first document, followed by pages 1-40 of the second and pages 1-40 of the third.

- which pages (or page ranges) you want printed

- whether you want to limit the print run to odd or even pages

- whether you want the print run restricted to text you selected before initiating printing

- whether you want the pages printed in reverse order (e.g. from the last page to the first)

- the quality of the eventual output (with many printers, Word allows you to print with minimal formatting for proofing purposes)

- whether you want to go on working in Word while the document prints (the default). Word calls this 'background printing'.

You can 'mix and match' these, as appropriate.

# Printing - the fast track approach

Since documents and printing needs vary dramatically, it's often necessary to customise print options before you begin printing.

For example, if you've created a document which contains numerous pictures, you may well want to print out a draft copy for proofing purposes prior to printing the final version (although Print Preview mode provides a very effective indication of how a document will look when printed, there are still errors which are only detectable when you're working with hard copy). In this situation, you may wish to exclude pictures or print with minimal formatting. (For how to set your own print options, see the 'Customised printing (1)' and 'Customised printing (2)' topics later).

On the other hand, simple documents can often benefit from a simple approach. In this case, you may well be content to print using the default options. Word recognises this and provides a method which bypasses the standard Print dialog, and is therefore much quicker and easier to use.

## Printing with the current print options

First, ensure your printer is ready and on-line. Make sure the Standard toolbar is visible. (If it isn't, pull down the View menu and click Toolbars, Standard). Now do the following:

Click here

Word starts printing the active document immediately.

# Customised printing (1)

If you need to set revised print options before printing, do the following.

**HANDY TIP**

**If you need to print in reverse order or with minimal formatting (or if you want to turn off background printing), follow the procedures under 'Customised printing (2)' before you carry out step 6 here.**

Pull down the File menu and click Print. Now carry out steps 1-5, as appropriate. Finally, carry out step 6.

1 Click here to deselect collation

2 Type in the number of copies

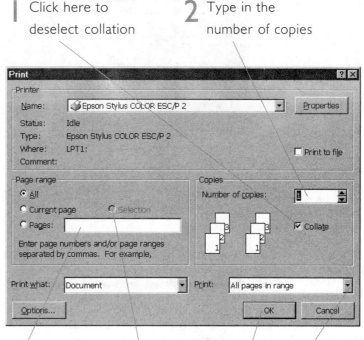

**HANDY TIP**

**Re step 3 – separate non-adjacent pages with commas but no spaces – e.g. to print pages 5, 12, 16 & 19 type in: '5,12,16,19'. Enter contiguous pages with dashes – e.g. to print pages 12 to 23 inclusive, type in: '12-23'. (Omit the quote marks in all examples.)**

3 Type in the relevant page range (see tip opposite)

4 Click here if you selected text before launching this dialog and this is all you want to print

6 Click here

5 To print only odd or even pages, click here; select Odd Pages or Even Pages.

Word starts printing the active document.

# Customised printing (2)

Other print options are accessible from within a special dialog. This is launched from within the Print dialog.

First, pull down the File menu and click Print. Then do the following:

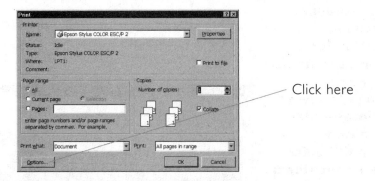

Click here

Now carry out steps 1-3 below, as appropriate. Then follow step 4.

| Click here to print with minimal formatting

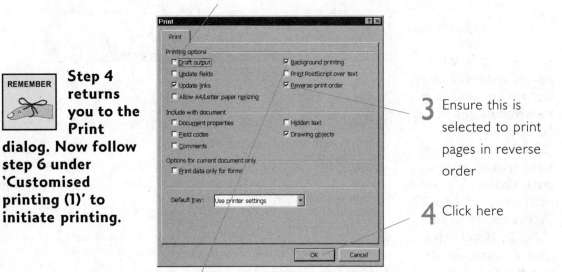

REMEMBER **Step 4 returns you to the Print dialog. Now follow step 6 under 'Customised printing (1)' to initiate printing.**

**3** Ensure this is selected to print pages in reverse order

**4** Click here

**2** Click here to turn off background printing

# Excel

This chapter gives you the fundamentals of using Excel. You'll learn how to work with data and formulas, and how to move around through worksheets. You'll also learn how to insert pictures, and make your data more visually effective by viewing it as a chart. Finally, you'll customise worksheet layout, preview your work and then print it out.

## Covers

Section Three

# The Excel screen

Below is a detailed illustration of the Excel screen.

**This is a floating toolbar, specific to the invoice worksheet:**

Title bar    Menu bar    Column letters

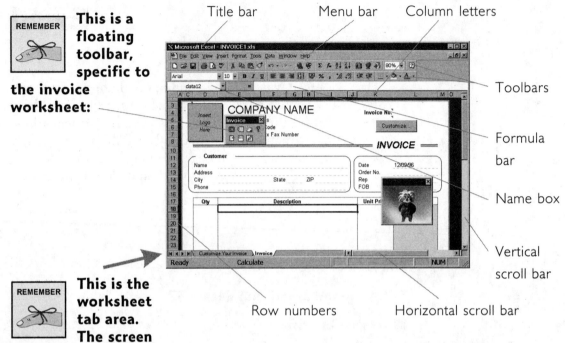

Toolbars

Formula bar

Name box

Vertical scroll bar

Row numbers    Horizontal scroll bar

**This is the worksheet tab area. The screen components here are used to move through Excel documents.**

Some of these screen components can be hidden at will.

## Specifying which screen components display

Pull down the Tools menu and click Options. Then:

Ensure the View tab is active

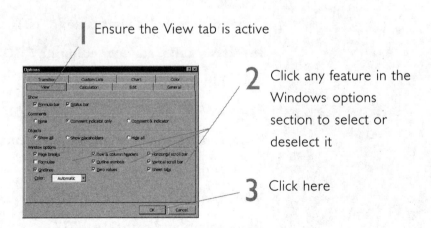

2 Click any feature in the Windows options section to select or deselect it

3 Click here

# Entering data (1)

When you start Excel, you're presented with a new blank spreadsheet:

**When you run Excel, you're actually opening a new workbook (see below). Excel calls these 'Book 1', 'Book 2' etc.**

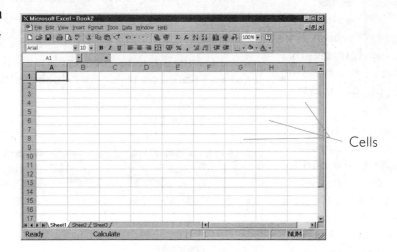

Cells

This means that you can start entering data immediately.

In Excel, you can enter the following basic data types:

- values (i.e. numbers)

- text (e.g. headings and explanatory material)

- functions (e.g. Sine or Cosine)

- formulas (combinations of values, text and functions)

**Columns are vertical, rows horizontal. Each worksheet can have as many as 256 columns and 65,536 rows, making a grand total of 16,777,216 cells.**

You enter data into 'cells'. Cells are formed where rows and columns intersect. In the figure above, cells H6, G8 and I4 are flagged for illustration purposes.

Collections of rows/columns and cells are known in Excel as worksheets. Worksheets are organised into workbooks (by default, each workbook has 3 worksheets). Workbooks are the files that are stored on disk when you save your work in Excel.

# Entering data (2)

**HANDY TIP**

**When you enter values which are too big (physically) to fit in the holding cell, Excel inserts:**
#####
**To resolve this, widen the column (see the 'Amending row/column sizes' topic later). Or pull down the Format menu and click Column, Autofit Selection to have Excel automatically increase the column size to match the contents.**

Although you can enter data *directly* into a cell (by simply clicking in the cell and typing it in), there's another method you can use which is often easier. Excel provides a special screen component known as the Formula bar.

The illustration below shows the end of a blank worksheet. Some sample text has been inserted into cell IV65536 (note that the Name box tells you which cell is currently active).

Name box

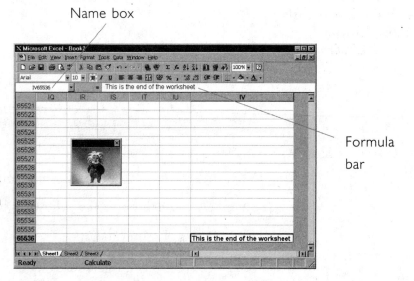

Formula bar

## Entering data via the Formula bar

Click the cell you want to insert data into. Then click the Formula bar. Type in the data. Then follow step 1 below. If you decide not to proceed with the operation, follow step 2 instead:

**HANDY TIP**

**You can use a keyboard route to confirm operations in the Formula bar: simply press Return.**

Click here

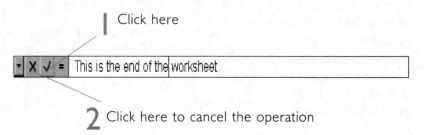

This is the end of the worksheet

2 Click here to cancel the operation

# Modifying existing data

**HANDY TIP**

**Excel now supports multiple undos and redos. To undo one or more editing actions, do the following:**

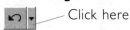 Click here

**in the Standard toolbar. Make your selection in the list and press Enter. To redo one or more actions, do the following:**

 Click here

**in the Standard toolbar. Make your selection in the list and press Enter.**

You can amend the contents of a cell in two ways:

* via the Formula bar

* from within the cell

When you use either of these methods, Excel enters a special state known as Edit Mode.

## Amending existing data using the Formula bar

Click the cell whose contents you want to change. Then click in the Formula bar. Make the appropriate revisions and/or additions. Then press Return. Excel updates the relevant cell.

## Amending existing data internally

Click the cell whose contents you want to change. Press F2. Make the appropriate revisions and/or additions *within the cell*. Then press Return.

The illustration below shows a section of a workbook created with the template INVOICE.XLT supplied with Excel.

A magnified view of cell K18, in Edit Mode

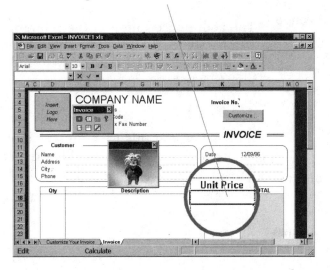

# Working with cell ranges

When you're working with more than one cell, it's often convenient and useful to organise them in 'ranges'.

A range is a rectangular arrangement of cells. In the illustration below, cells A3, A4, A5, A6, B3, B4, B5 and B6 have been selected.

A selected cell range

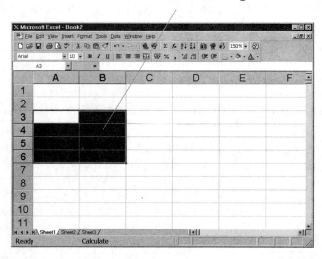

**You can also use additional reference shortcuts (use the following as guides):**
**All cells in row 15:**
*15:15*
**All cells in rows 8 to 20:**
*8:20*
**All cells in column A:**
*A:A*
**All cells in columns P to S:**
*P:S.*

The above description of the relevant cells is very cumbersome. It's much more useful to use a form of shorthand. Excel (using the start and end cells as reference points) refers to these cells as:

A3:B6

You can extend this even more. Cell addresses can also incorporate a component which refers to the worksheet that contains the range. For example, to denote that the range A3:B6 is in worksheet 8, you'd use:

Sheet8!A3:B6

# Moving around in worksheets (1)

Excel worksheets are huge. Moving to cells which happen to be visible is easy: you simply click in the relevant cell. However, Excel provides several techniques you can use to jump to less accessible areas.

## Using the scroll bars

Use any of the following methods:

**When you carry out steps 1 and 2 on the right, Excel displays a bubble showing where you're up to:**

Row: 13

1. to scroll quickly to another section of the active worksheet, drag the scroll box along the scroll bar until you reach it

2. to move one window to the right or left, click to the left or right of the scroll box in the horizontal scroll bar

3. to move one window up or down, click above or below the scroll box in the vertical scroll bar

4. to move up or down by one row, click the arrows in the vertical scroll bar

5. to move left or right by one column, click the arrows in the horizontal scroll bar

Scroll boxes

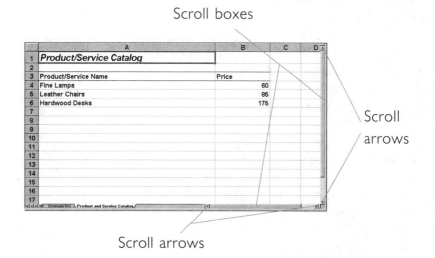

Scroll arrows

Scroll arrows

# Moving around in worksheets (2)

**Excel facilitates worksheet navigation.** As you move the insertion point from cell to cell, the relevant row and column headers are emboldened:

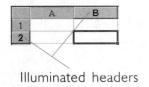

Illuminated headers

**You can use a keyboard shortcut to launch the Go To dialog: simply press F5, or Ctrl+G.**

**Re step 1 - a cell's 'reference' (or 'address') identifies it in relation to its position in a worksheet, e.g. BII or H23. You can also type in cell ranges here.**

## Using the keyboard
You can use the following techniques:

1.  use the cursor keys to move one cell left, right, up or down.

2.  hold down Ctrl as you use 1. above; this jumps to the edge of the current section (e.g. if cell BII is active and you hold down Ctrl as you press ➜, Excel jumps to IVII, the last cell in row II).

3.  press Home to jump to the first cell in the active row, or Ctrl+Home to move to AI.

4.  press Page Up or Page Down to move up or down by one screen.

5.  press Alt+Page Down to move one screen to the right, or Alt+Page Up to move one screen to the left.

## Using the Go To dialog
Excel provides a special dialog which you can use to specify precise cell destinations.

Pull down the Edit menu and click Go To. Now do the following:

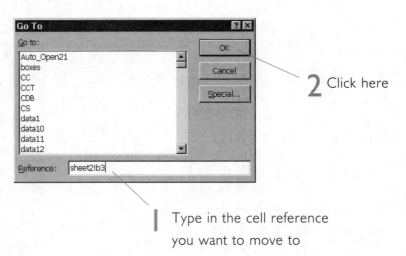

2 Click here

Type in the cell reference you want to move to

# Switching between worksheets

Because workbooks have more than one worksheet, Excel provides two easy and convenient methods for moving between them.

### Using the Tab area

You can use the Tab area (at the base of the Excel screen) to:

- jump to the first or last sheet

- jump to the next or previous sheet

- jump to a specific sheet

See the illustration below:

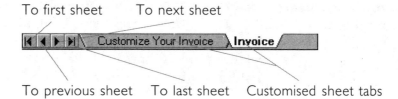

To first sheet    To next sheet

To previous sheet    To last sheet    Customised sheet tabs

To move to a specific sheet, simply click the relevant tab.

An example: in the illustration above, to jump to the 'Customize Your Invoice' worksheet, simply click the appropriate tab.

When you click a worksheet tab, Excel emboldens the name and makes the tab background white.

### Using the keyboard

You can use a keyboard shortcut here.

*Ctrl+Page Up*        moves to the previous tab

*Ctrl+Page Down*      moves to the next tab

# Other operations on worksheets (1)

We said earlier that, by default, each workbook has 3 worksheets. However, you can easily:

- add new worksheets

- delete existing worksheets

- move existing worksheets

### Inserting a single worksheet

In the worksheet tab area at the base of the screen, click the tab which represents the sheet in front of which you want the new worksheet inserted. Pull down the Insert menu and click Worksheet.

**HANDY TIP** **You can use a keyboard shortcut to insert a worksheet: simply press Shift+F11.**

### Inserting more than one worksheet

To add multiple worksheets, hold down one Shift key as you click the required number of sheet tabs (in other words, to add 6 new worksheets, shift-click 6 tabs). Then pull down the Insert menu and click Worksheet.

### Deleting worksheets

In the worksheet tab area, click a single worksheet tab (or shift-click multiple tabs to delete more than one worksheet at a time). Pull down the Edit menu and click Delete Sheet. Excel launches a special message. Do the following:

**BEWARE** **When you delete a worksheet, you automatically erase the worksheet contents, too.**

Click here to proceed
with the deletion

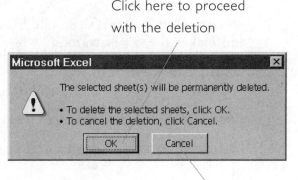

Or here to cancel it and
return to your workbook

# Other operations on worksheets (2)

You can perform two kinds of move operation on worksheets. You can:

- rearrange the worksheet order within a given workbook

- transfer a worksheet to another workbook

## Rearranging worksheets

To select a single worksheet, click the relevant sheet tab in the worksheet tab area. Or select more than one worksheet by holding down one Shift key as you click multiple tabs. With the mouse pointer still over the selected tab(s), hold down the left mouse button and drag them to their new location. Release the mouse button to confirm the operation.

## Moving worksheets to another workbook

To select a single worksheet, click the relevant sheet tab in the worksheet tab area. Or select more than one worksheet by holding down one Shift key as you click multiple tabs. Pull down the Edit menu and click Move or Copy Sheet. Now do the following:

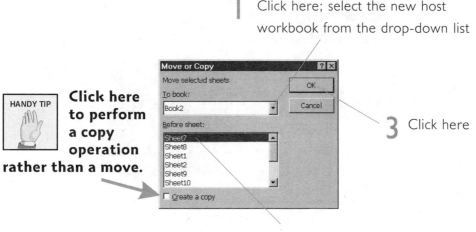

**1** Click here; select the new host workbook from the drop-down list

**3** Click here

**HANDY TIP** **Click here to perform a copy operation rather than a move.**

**2** Click the worksheet in front of which you want the transferred sheet(s) to appear

# Selection techniques (1)

Before you can carry out any editing operations on cells in Excel, you have to select them first. Selecting a single cell is very easy: you merely click in it. However, Excel provides a variety of selection techniques which you can use to select more than one cell.

**With the exception of the first cell, a selected range is filled with black.**

## Selecting adjacent cell ranges

The easiest way to do this is to use the mouse. Click in the first cell in the range; hold down the left mouse button and drag over the remaining cells. Release the mouse button.

You can use the keyboard, too. Position the cell pointer over the first cell in the range. Hold down one Shift key as you use the relevant cursor key to extend the selection. Release the keys when the correct selection has been defined.

**You can use another keyboard route. Place the cell pointer in the first cell. Press F8. Use the cursor keys to define the selection. Finally, press F8 again.**

## Selecting separate cell ranges

Excel lets you select more than one range at a time. Look at the illustration below:

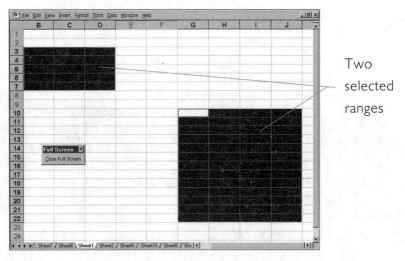

Two selected ranges

To select joint ranges, select the first in the normal way (you can't use the 'F8' method here). Then hold down Ctrl as you select subsequent ranges.

# Selection techniques (2)

### Selecting a single row or column
To select every cell within a row or column automatically, click on the row or column heading.

Column heading

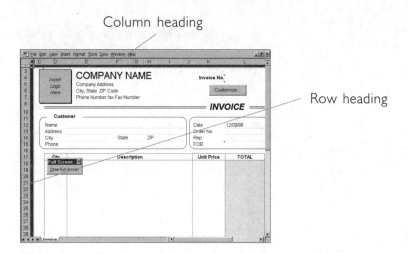

Row heading

### Selecting multiple rows or columns
To select more than one row or column, click on a row or column heading. Hold down the left mouse button and drag to select adjacent rows or columns.

### Selecting an entire worksheet
Click the Select All button:

**HANDY TIP** **You can use a keyboard shortcut to select every cell automatically: simply press Ctrl+A.**

A magnified view of the Select All button

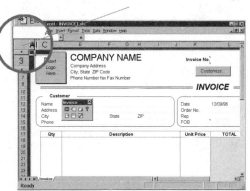

# Formulas - an overview

Formulas are cell entries which define how other values relate to each other.

As a very simple example, consider the following:

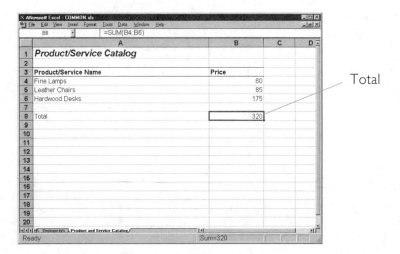

Total

Here, a cell has been defined which returns the total of cells B4:B6. Obviously, in this instance you could insert the total easily enough yourself because the individual values are so small, and because we're only dealing with a small number of cells. But what happens if the cell values are larger and/or more numerous, or – more to the point – if they're liable to change frequently?

The answer is to insert a formula which carries out the necessary calculation automatically.

If you look at the Formula bar in the illustration, you'll see the formula which does this:

=SUM(B4:B6)

Many Excel formulas are much more complex than this, but the principles remain the same.

# Inserting a formula

**Arguments (e.g. cell references) relating to functions are always contained in brackets.**

All formulas in Excel begin with an equals sign. This is usually followed by a permutation of the following:

- an operand (cell reference, e.g. B4)

- a function (e.g. the summation function, SUM)

- an arithmetical operator (+, −, / and *)

- comparison operators (<, >, <=, >= and =)

Excel supports a very wide range of functions organised into numerous categories. For more information on how to insert functions, see the 'Inserting a function' topic.

The mathematical operators are (in the order in which they appear in the bulleted list): *plus, minus, divide* and *multiply.*

**To enter the same formula into a cell range, select the range, type the formula and then press CTRL+ENTER.**

The comparison operators are (in the order in which they appear in the list): *less than, greater than, less than or equal to, greater than or equal to* and *equals.*

There are two ways to enter formulas:

## Entering a formula directly into the cell

Click the cell in which you want to insert a formula. Then type =, followed by your formula. When you've finished, press Return.

## Entering a formula into the Formula bar

This is usually the most convenient method.

Click the cell in which you want to insert a formula. Then click in the Formula bar. Type =, followed by your formula. When you've finished, press Return or do the following:

Click here

# Inserting a function

Functions are pre-defined tools which accomplish specific tasks. These tasks are often calculations; occasionally, however, they're more generalised (e.g. some functions simply return dates and/or times). In effect, functions replace one or more formulas.

HANDY TIP **Excel organises its functions under convenient headings (e.g. Financial, Date & Time, Statistical and Text).**

Excel provides a special dialog – the Formula Palette – to help ensure that you enter functions correctly. This is useful for the following reasons:

* Excel provides so many functions, it's convenient to apply them from a centralised source

* the Formula Palette ensures the functions are entered with the correct syntax

Functions can only be used in formulas.

### Inserting a function with the Formula Palette

At the relevant juncture during the process of inserting a formula, refer to the Formula bar and do the following:

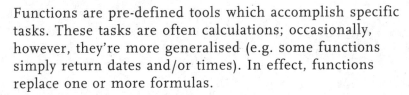
— Click here

HANDY TIP **You can also use another route to insert a function. Click in a cell. Pull down the Insert menu and click Function. In the Function category field in the Paste Function dialog, select a heading. Click a function in the Function name box. Click OK. Excel now launches the Formula Palette – complete steps 2 and 3.**

Now carry out the following steps:

Click here; select a function from the list

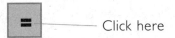

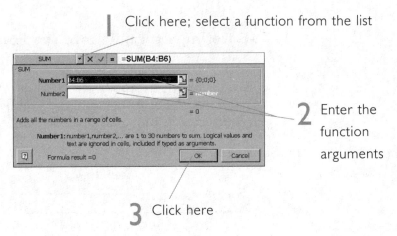

2 Enter the function arguments

3 Click here

# Amending row/column sizes

Sooner or later, you'll find it necessary to change the width of rows or columns. This necessity arises when there is too much data in cells to display adequately. You can enlarge or shrink single or multiple rows/columns.

### Changing row height

To change one row's height, click the row heading. If you want to change multiple rows, hold down Ctrl and click the appropriate extra headings. Then place the mouse pointer over the line located just under the row heading(s). Hold down the left mouse button and drag the line up or down to decrease or increase the row(s) respectively. Release the mouse button to confirm the operation.

**Excel has a useful 'best fit' feature. Simply double-click the line below the selected row headings, or to the right of selected column headings, to have the rows or columns adjust themselves automatically to their contents.**

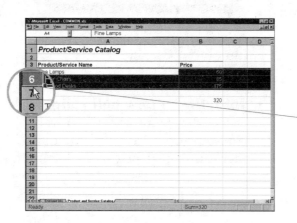

A magnified view of the line to drag if you're amending rows 4, 5 and 6 jointly

### Changing column width

To change one column's width, click the column heading. If you want to change multiple columns, hold down Ctrl and click the appropriate extra headings. Then place the mouse pointer over the line located just to the right of the column heading(s). Hold down the left mouse button and drag the line right or left to widen or narrow the column(s) respectively.

Release the mouse button to confirm the operation.

# Inserting cells, rows or columns

You can insert additional cells, rows or columns into worksheets.

### Inserting a new row or column

First, select one or more cells within the row(s) or column(s) where you want to carry out the insert operation. Now pull down the Insert menu and click Rows or Columns, as appropriate. Excel inserts the new row(s) or column(s) immediately.

**If you select cells in more than one row or column, Excel inserts the equivalent number of new rows or columns.**

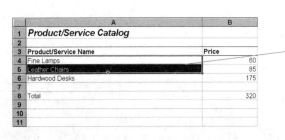

A worksheet extract. Here, one new column or two new rows are being added

### Inserting a new cell range

Select the range where you want to insert the new cells. Pull down the Insert menu and click Cells. Now carry out step 1 or step 2 below. Finally, follow step 3.

**1** Click here to have Excel make room for the new cells by moving the selected range *to the right*

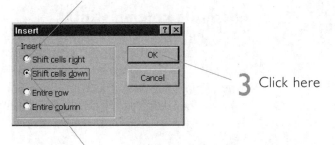

**3** Click here

**2** Click here to have Excel make room for the new cells by moving the selected range *down*

# AutoFill

Excel lets you insert data series automatically. This is a very useful and timesaving feature. Look at the illustration below:

**Types of series you can use AutoFill to complete include: 1st Period, 2nd Period etc.; Mon, Tue, Wed etc.; Quarter 1, Quarter 2 etc.; Week1, Week2, Week 3 etc.**

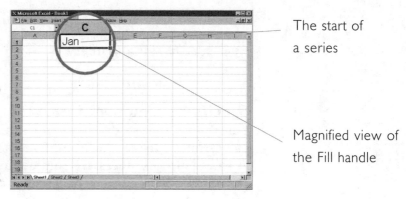

The start of a series

Magnified view of the Fill handle

If you wanted to insert month names in successive cells in column A, you could do so manually. But there's a much easier way. You can use Excel's AutoFill feature.

## Using AutoFill to create a series

Type in the first element(s) of the series in consecutive cells. Select the cells. Then position the mouse pointer over the Fill handle in the bottom right-hand corner of the last cell (the pointer changes to a crosshair). Hold down the left mouse button and drag the handle over the cells into which you want to extend the series (in the example here, over C2:C12). When you release the mouse button, Excel extrapolates the initial entry or entries into the appropriate series.

| | A | B | C |
|---|---|---|---|
| 1 | | | Jan |
| 2 | | | Feb |
| 3 | | | Mar |
| 4 | | | Apr |
| 5 | | | May |
| 6 | | | Jun |
| 7 | | | Jul |
| 8 | | | Aug |
| 9 | | | Sep |
| 10 | | | Oct |
| 11 | | | Nov |
| 12 | | | Dec |

The completed series

# Changing number formats

Excel lets you apply formatting enhancements to cells and their contents. You can:

- specify a number format

- customise the font, type size and style of contents

- specify cell alignment

- border and/or shade cells

### Specifying a number format

You can customise the way cell contents (e.g. numbers and dates/times) display in Excel. For example, you can specify at what point numbers are rounded up. Available formats are organised under several general categories. These include: Number, Accounting and Fraction.

Select the cells whose contents you want to customise. Pull down the Format menu and click Cells. Now do the following:

**Re step 3 –** **the** **options** **you can** **choose from vary** **according to the** **category chosen.** **Complete them as** **necessary.**

1 Ensure the Number tab is active

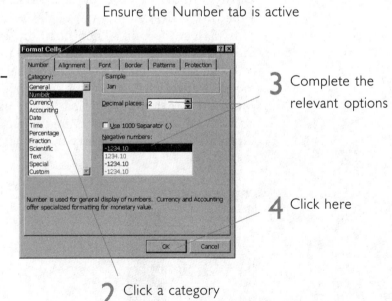

3 Complete the relevant options

4 Click here

2 Click a category

# Changing fonts and styles

Excel lets you carry out the following actions on cell contents (numbers and/or text):

- apply a new font and/or type size

- apply a font style (for most fonts, you can choose from: Regular, Italic, Bold or Bold Italic)

- apply a colour

- apply a special effect (underlining, ~~strikethrough~~, superscript or subscript)

## Amending the appearance of cell contents

Select the cell(s) whose contents you want to reformat. Pull down the Format menu and click Cells. Carry out step 1 below. Now follow any of steps 2-5, as appropriate, or either or both of the two tips. Finally, carry out step 6.

**HANDY TIP**

**To underline the specified contents, click the arrow to the right of the Underline box; select an underlining type in the list.**

**HANDY TIP**

**To apply a special effect, click any of the options in the Effects section.**

1 Ensure the Font tab is active

3 Type in a type size

5 Click the style you want to apply

6 Click here

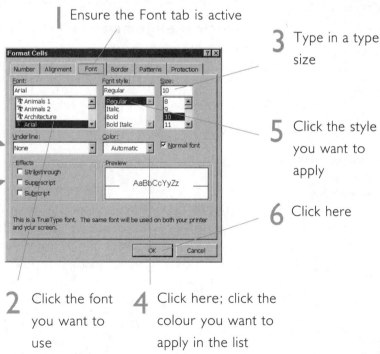

2 Click the font you want to use

4 Click here; click the colour you want to apply in the list

# Cell alignment (1)

By default, Excel aligns text to the left of cells, and numbers to the right. However, if you want you can change this.

You can specify alignment under two broad headings: Horizontal and Vertical.

## Horizontal alignment

The main options are:

**REMEMBER**

**One further horizontal option - Center across selection - centres cell contents across more than one cell (if you selected a cell range before initiating it).**

| | |
|---|---|
| *General* | the default (see above) |
| *Left* | contents are aligned from the left |
| *Center* | contents are centred |
| *Right* | contents are aligned from the right |
| *Fill* | contents are duplicated so that they fill the cell |
| *Justify* | a combination of Left and Right. |

## Vertical alignment

Available options are:

**HANDY TIP**

**You can also rotate text within cells – see 'Cell alignment (2)' for more information.**

| | |
|---|---|
| *Top* | cell contents align with the top of the cell(s) |
| *Center* | contents are centred |
| *Bottom* | contents align with the cell bottom |
| *Justify* | contents are aligned along the top and bottom of the cell(s) |

Most of these settings parallel features found in Word (and many other word-processors). The difference, however, lies in the fact that Excel has to align data within the bounds of cells rather than a page. When it aligns text, it often needs to employ its own version of text wrap. See 'Cell alignment (2)' for more information on this.

# Cell alignment (2)

Other alignment features you can set are rotation and text wrap.

Rotation controls the direction of text flow within cells; you achieve this by specifying a plus (anticlockwise) or minus (clockwise) angle.

When the Wrap Text option is selected, Excel – instead of overflowing any surplus text into adjacent cells to the right – forces it onto separate lines within the host cell.

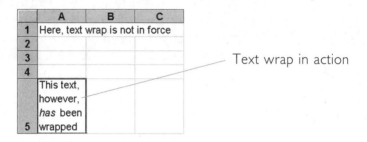

Text wrap in action

## Customising cell alignment

Select the cell(s) whose contents you want to realign. Pull down the Format menu and click Cells. Carry out step 1 below. Now follow any or all of steps 2-4, as appropriate. Finally, carry out step 5.

1 | Ensure the Alignment tab is active

**Click here to wrap text within the holding cell(s):**

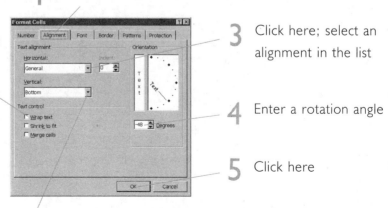

3 Click here; select an alignment in the list

4 Enter a rotation angle

5 Click here

2 Click here; select an alignment in the list

# Bordering cells

Excel lets you define a border around:

- the perimeter of a selected cell range

- specific sides within a cell range

You can customise the border by choosing from a selection of pre-defined border styles. You can also colour the border, if required.

### Applying a cell border

First, select the cell range you want to border. Pull down the Format menu and click Cells. Now carry out steps 1 and 2 below. Step 3 is optional. Follow steps 4 and 5, as appropriate (if you're setting *multiple* border options, repeat steps 2-5 as required). Finally, carry out step 6:

1 Ensure the Border tab is active

4 Click the relevant border style option

**Re step 5 – clicking any of the indicated buttons borders just one side.**

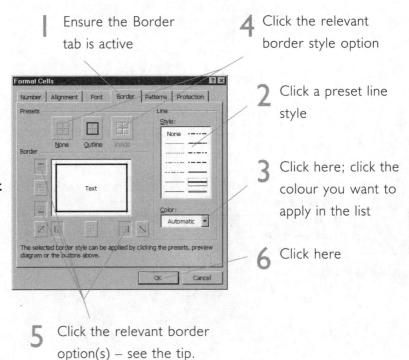

2 Click a preset line style

3 Click here; click the colour you want to apply in the list

6 Click here

5 Click the relevant border option(s) – see the tip.

# Shading cells

Excel lets you apply the following to cells:

- a pattern

- a pattern colour

- a background colour

You can do any of these singly, or in combination. Interesting effects can be achieved by using pattern colours with coloured backgrounds.

## Applying a pattern or background

First, select the cell range you want to shade. Pull down the Format menu and click Cells. Now carry out step 1. Perform step 2 to apply a *background* colour, and/or 3-4 to apply a *foreground* pattern or pattern/colour combination. Finally, follow step 5.

**HANDY TIP**

**The Sample field previews** how your background and pattern/colour will look.

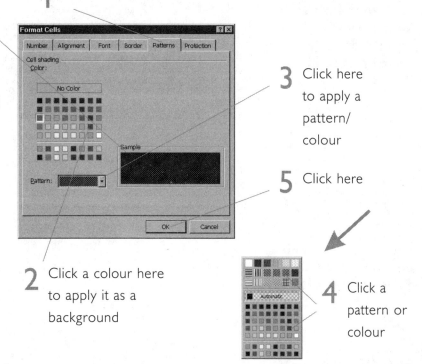

1 Ensure the Patterns tab is active

3 Click here to apply a pattern/ colour

5 Click here

2 Click a colour here to apply it as a background

4 Click a pattern or colour

# AutoFormat

Excel provides a shortcut to the formatting of worksheet data: AutoFormat.

AutoFormat consists of 16 pre-defined formatting schemes. These incorporate specific excerpts from the font, number, alignment, border and shading options discussed earlier. You can apply any of these schemes (and their associated formatting) to selected cell ranges with just a few mouse clicks. You can even specify which scheme elements you *don't* wish to use.

AutoFormat works with most arrangements of worksheet data.

### Using AutoFormat

First, select the cell range you want to apply an automatic format to. Pull down the Format menu and click AutoFormat. Now carry out step 1 below. Steps 2 and 3 are optional. Finally, follow step 4.

**HANDY TIP**

**The Sample field previews how your data will look with the specified AutoFormat.**

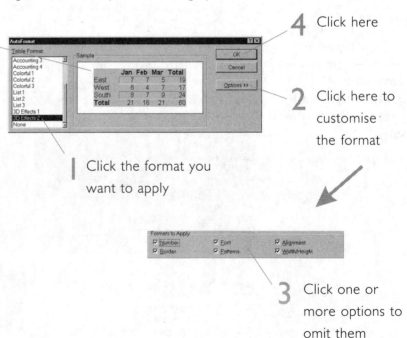

4 Click here

2 Click here to customise the format

Click the format you want to apply

**REMEMBER**

**Re step 3 - the dialog shown here is an addition to the AutoFormat dialog.**

3 Click one or more options to omit them

# Find operations

Excel lets you search for and jump to text or numbers (in short, any information) in your worksheets. This is a particularly useful feature when worksheets become large and complex.

You can organise your search by rows or by columns. You can also specify whether Excel looks in:

- cells that contain formulas

- cells that don't contain formulas

Additionally, you can insist that Excel only flag exact matches (i.e. if you searched for '11', Excel would not find '1111'), and you can also limit text searches to text which has the case you specified (e.g. searching for 'PRODUCT LIST' would not find 'Product List').

## Searching for data

Place the mouse pointer at the location in the active worksheet from which you want the search to begin. Pull down the Edit menu and click Find. Now carry out step 1 below, then any of steps 2-5. Finally, carry out step 6.

**To search for data over more than one worksheet, select the relevant sheet tabs before following steps 1-6.**

**If you want to restrict the search to specific cells, select a cell range *before* you follow steps 1-6.**

1 Type in the data you want to find

4 Click here for a case-specific search

6 Click here

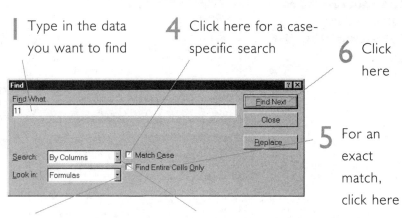

5 For an exact match, click here

2 To limit the search, click here; select the relevant option from the list

3 To specify the search direction, click here; select the relevant option from the list

# Find-and-replace operations

When you search for data, you can also – if you want – have Excel replace it with something else.

Find-and-replace operations can be organised by rows or by columns. However, unlike straight searches, you can't specify whether Excel looks in cells that contain formulas or those that don't. As with straight searches, you can, however, limit find-and-replace operations to exact matches and also (in the case of text) to precise case matches.

Normally, find-and-replace operations only affect the worksheet in which they're conducted. If you want to carry out an operation over multiple worksheets, see the tip.

### Running a find-and-replace operation

Place the mouse pointer at the location in the active worksheet from which you want the search to begin (or select a cell range if you want to restrict the find-and-replace operation to this). Pull down the Edit menu and click Replace. Now carry out step 1 below, then any of steps 2-5. Finally, carry out step 6, and steps 7 and/or 8 as required.

**To search for and replace data over more than one worksheet, select the relevant sheet tabs before following steps 1-8.**

1 Type in the data you want to find

4 Click here for a case-specific search

6 Click here to find the 1st occurrence

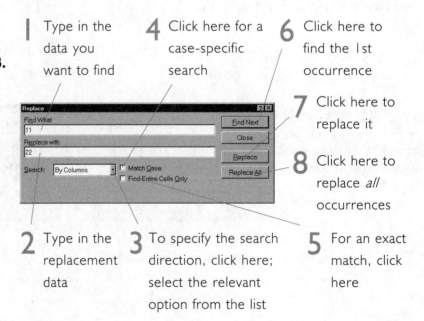

7 Click here to replace it

8 Click here to replace *all* occurrences

2 Type in the replacement data

3 To specify the search direction, click here; select the relevant option from the list

5 For an exact match, click here

# Charting - an overview

Excel has comprehensive charting capabilities. You can have it convert selected data into its visual equivalent. To do this, Excel offers a wide number of chart formats and sub-formats.

You can create a chart:

- as a picture within the parent worksheet

- as a separate chart sheet

Chart sheets have their own tabs in the tab area; these operate just like worksheet tabs.

Excel uses a special Wizard – ChartWizard – to make the process of creating charts as easy and convenient as possible.

**HANDY TIP**

**You can add a picture to chart walls. Select the wall(s) in the normal way. Then follow the procedures set out on page 116.**

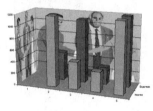

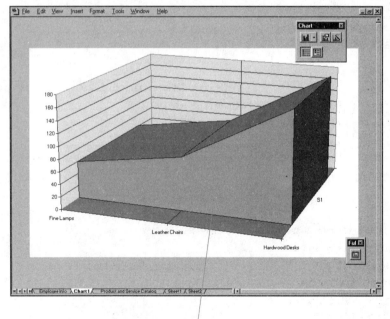

A 3-D Area chart

# Creating a chart (1)

**Click and hold here to have Excel preview the chart type/sub-type combination:**

First, select the cells you want converted into a chart. Pull down the Insert menu and click Chart. The first ChartWizard dialog appears. Do the following:

Click a chart type

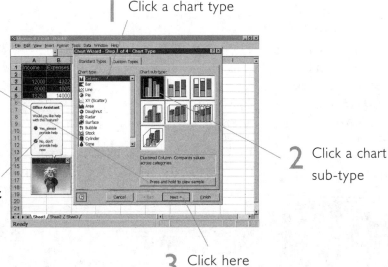

**Click here: if you want the Office Assistant to supply help with chart creation.**

**2** Click a chart sub-type

**3** Click here

There are three more dialogs to complete. Carry out the following steps:

**Re step 4 – click the Collapse Dialog button:**

to hide the dialog temporarily while you select an alternative cell range. When you've finished, do the following:

Click here

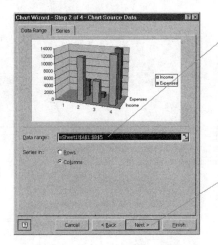

**4** If you selected the wrong cells before launching the Chart Wizard, click here; then select the correct range in your worksheet

**5** Click here

# Creating a chart (2)

Excel launches the third ChartWizard dialog. Carry out the following steps:

**Click any of the additional tabs to set further chart options. For example, activate the Gridlines tab to specify how and where gridlines display. Or click Legend to determine where legends (text labels) display...**

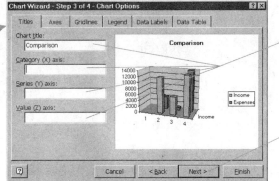

I Optional – name the chart and/or axes

2 Click here

In the final dialog, you tell Excel whether you want the chart inserted into the current worksheet, or into a new chart sheet.

Carry out step 3 OR 4 below. Finally, perform step 5.

3 Click here to create a chart sheet

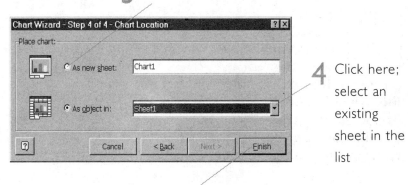

4 Click here; select an existing sheet in the list

5 Click here to generate the chart

# Working with pictures

Most worksheets benefit from the inclusion of colour or greyscale pictures. These can be:

**HANDY TIP**

**Once inserted into a worksheet,** pictures can be resized and moved in the normal way.

- output from other programs (e.g. drawings and illustrations)

- commercial clip art

- photographs

Excel will happily translate a wide variety of third-party graphics formats.

### Inserting a picture

**HANDY TIP**

**You can also insert pictures onto chart** walls – see page 113.

Position the insertion point at the location in the active worksheet where you want the picture to appear. Pull down the Insert menu and click Picture, From File. Now carry out the following steps:

**2** Click here. In the drop-down list, click the drive/folder which hosts the picture

**4** Click here

**REMEMBER**

**Excel provides a preview of what the** picture will look like when it's been imported. See the Preview box on the right of the dialog.

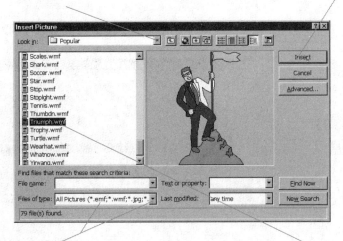

**1** Make sure All Pictures is shown. If it isn't, click the arrow and select it from the drop-down list

**3** Click a picture file

# Page setup - an overview

**Excel has a special view mode: – Page Break Preview – which you can also use to ensure your worksheet prints correctly. Pull down the View menu and click Page Break Preview. Do the following (the white area denotes cells which will print, the grey those which won't):**

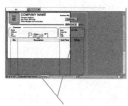

Drag page break margins to customise the printable area

**Charts in separate chart sheets have unique page setup options - see later.**

Making sure your worksheets print with the correct page setup can be a complex issue, for the simple reason that most worksheets become very extensive with the passage of time (so large, in fact, that in the normal course of things they won't fit onto a single page).

Page setup features you can customise include:

- the paper size and orientation

- scaling

- the starting page number

- the print quality

- margins

- header/footer information

- page order

- which worksheet components print

Margin settings you can amend are:

- top

- bottom

- left

- right

Additionally, you can set the distance between the top page edge and the top of the header, and the distance between the bottom page edge and the bottom edge of the footer.

When you save your active workbook, all Page Setup settings are saved with it.

# Setting page options

Excel comes with some 17 pre-defined paper sizes which you can apply to your worksheets, in either portrait (top-to-bottom) or landscape (sideways on) orientation. This is one approach to effective printing. Another is scaling: you can print out your worksheets as they are, or you can have Excel shrink them so that they fit a given paper size (you can even automate this process). Additionally, you can set the print resolution and starting page number.

### Using the Page tab in the Page Setup dialog

Pull down the File menu and click Page Setup. Now carry out step 1 below, followed by steps 2-6 as appropriate. Finally, carry out step 7:

**HANDY TIP**

**Re step 5 – by default, Excel numbers pages from '1'. Leave the First Page Number field setting as Auto if you want this.**

1 Ensure the Page tab is active

2 Click the orientation you need

3 Click here; click the page size you need in the drop-down list

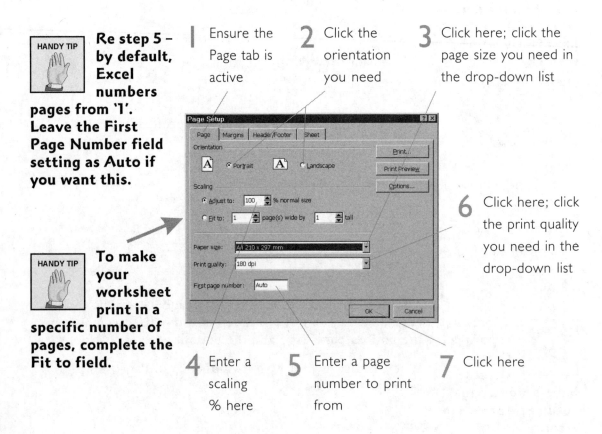

**HANDY TIP**

**To make your worksheet print in a specific number of pages, complete the Fit to field.**

6 Click here; click the print quality you need in the drop-down list

4 Enter a scaling % here

5 Enter a page number to print from

7 Click here

# Setting margin options

Excel lets you set a variety of margin settings. The illustration below shows the main ones:

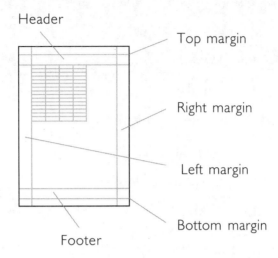

Header

Top margin

Right margin

Left margin

Bottom margin

Footer

## Using the Margins tab in the Page Setup dialog

Pull down the File menu and click Page Setup. Now carry out step 1 below, followed by steps 2-3 as appropriate. Finally, carry out step 4:

1 Ensure the Margins tab is active

**HANDY TIP**

**To specify how your worksheet aligns on the page, click either option here:**

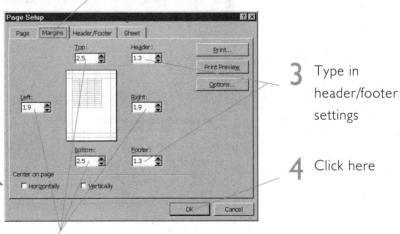

3 Type in header/footer settings

4 Click here

2 Type in the margin settings you need

# Setting header/footer options

Excel provides a list of built-in header and footer settings. You can apply any of these to the active worksheet. These settings include:

- the worksheet title

- the workbook title

- the date

- the user's name

- 'confidential'

- permutations of these

## Using the Header/Footer tab in the Page Setup dialog

Pull down the File menu and click Page Setup. Now carry out step 1 below, followed by steps 2-3 as appropriate. Finally, carry out step 4:

1 | Ensure the Header/Footer tab is active

2 Click here; select a header from the list

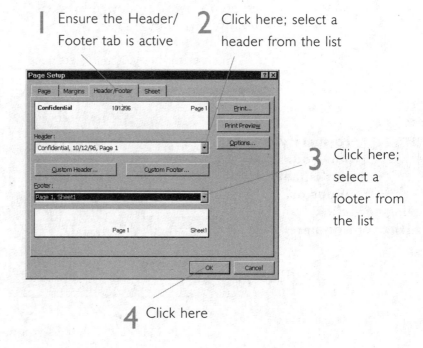

3 Click here; select a footer from the list

4 Click here

# Setting sheet options

Excel lets you:

- define a printable area on-screen

- define a column or row title which will print on every page

- specify which worksheet components should print

- print with minimal formatting

- determine the print direction

## Using the Sheet tab in the Page Setup dialog

Pull down the File menu and click Page Setup. Now carry out step 1 below, followed by steps 2-4 (and the tips) as appropriate. Finally, carry out step 5.

**If you want to print a specific cell range (area), type in the address here:**

**Click Draft Quality for rapid printing with the minimum of formatting.**

1 | Ensure the Sheet tab is active

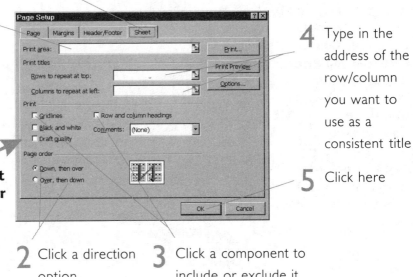

4 Type in the address of the row/column you want to use as a consistent title

5 Click here

2 Click a direction option

3 Click a component to include or exclude it

# Page setup for charts

Most page setup issues for charts in chart sheets are identical to those for worksheet data. The main difference, however, is that the Page Setup dialog has a Chart tab (rather than a Sheet tab).

In the Chart tab, you can opt to have the chart

- printed at full size

- scaled to fit the page

- user-defined

You can also set the print quality.

### Using the Chart tab in the Page Setup dialog

Click the relevant chart tab in the worksheet tab area. Pull down the File menu and click Page Setup. Now carry out step 1 below, followed by steps 2-3 as appropriate. Finally, carry out step 4.

**Re step 3 – clicking Custom ensures that, when you return to the chart sheet, the chart size can be adjusted with the mouse in the normal way. The chart then prints at whatever size you set.**

 Ensure the Chart tab is active

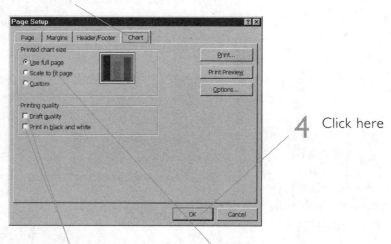

4 Click here

2 Click either option here to limit the print quality

3 Click any scale option here (see the tip)

# Launching Print Preview

Excel provides a special view mode called Print Preview. This displays the active worksheet exactly as it will look when printed. Use Print Preview as a final check just before you begin printing.

You can perform the following actions from within Print Preview:

- moving from page to page

- zooming in or out on the active page

- adjusting most Page Setup settings

- adjusting margins visually

**Excel's Print Preview mode has only two Zoom settings: Full Page and High-Magnification.**

### Launching Print Preview

Pull down the File menu and click Print Preview. This is the result:

**To leave Print Preview mode and return to your worksheet (or chart sheet), simply press Esc.**

Special Print Preview toolbar

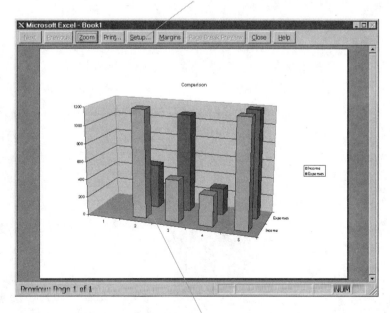

A preview of a chart sheet

# Working with Print Preview

All of the operations you can perform in Print Preview mode can be accessed via the toolbar.

**Click the Page Break Preview button to launch this view – see page 117 for how to use it.**

## Using the Print Preview toolbar

Do any of the following, as appropriate:

**1** Click here to jump to the next page

**3** Click here to zoom in or out

**6** Click here to launch the Page Setup dialog

**Re step 6 – see earlier topics (pages 117-122) for how to use the Page Setup dialog.**

| Next | Previous | Zoom | Print... | Setup... | Margins | Page Break Preview | Close | Help |

**2** Click here to jump to the previous page

**4** Click here to toggle margin markers on or off – then follow step 5

**5** Drag any margin to reposition it

Product and Service Catalog

**Product/Service Catalog**

Product/Service Name
Fine Lamps
Leather Chairs
Hardwood Desks

Page 1

# Printing worksheet data

Excel lets you specify:

- the number of copies you want printed

- whether you want the copies 'collated'. This is the process whereby Excel prints one full copy at a time. For instance, if you're printing three copies of a 10-page worksheet, Excel prints pages 1-10 of the first copy, followed by pages 1-10 of the second and pages 1-10 of the third.

- which pages (or page ranges) you want printed

- whether you want the print run restricted to cells you selected before initiating printing

You can 'mix and match' these, as appropriate.

**REMEMBER**

**To select and print more than one worksheet, hold down Shift as you click on multiple tabs in the worksheet tab area.**

## Starting a print run

Open the workbook that contains the data you want to print. If you want to print an entire worksheet, click the relevant tab in the worksheet tab area. If you need to print a specific cell range within a worksheet, select it. Then pull down the File menu and click Print. Do any of steps 1-5. Then carry out step 6 to begin printing.

**HANDY TIP**

**If you need to adjust your printer's internal settings before you initiate printing, click Properties. Then refer to your printer's manual.**

Click here; select the printer you want from the list

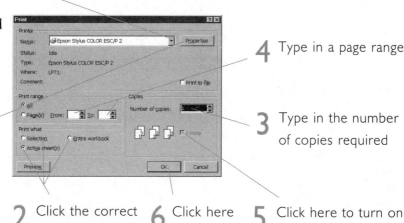

4 Type in a page range

3 Type in the number of copies required

2 Click the correct selection option

6 Click here

5 Click here to turn on collation

# Printing - the fast track approach

In earlier topics, we looked at how to customise print options to meet varying needs and worksheet sizes. However, Excel – like Word – recognises that there will be times when you won't need this level of complexity. There are occasions when you'll merely want to print out your work – often for proofing purposes – with the standard print defaults applying, and with the absolute minimum of mouse actions.

The default print options are:

- Excel prints only the active worksheet

- Excel prints only 1 copy

- Excel prints all pages within the active worksheet

- collation is turned off

For this reason, Excel provides a method which bypasses the standard Print dialog, and is therefore much quicker and easier to use.

## Printing with the default print options

First, click the tab that relates to the worksheet you want to print. Ensure your printer is ready. Make sure the Standard toolbar is visible. (If it isn't, pull down the View menu and click Toolbars, Standard.) Now do the following:

Click here

Excel starts printing the active worksheet immediately.

# PowerPoint

Use this chapter to acquire the basics of producing your own slide show. You'll use the AutoContent Wizard to automate the creation of a presentation, and learn how to customise it for your own use later. You'll run PowerPoint Central (for on-line tips and extra features) and use views to maximise your work. You'll automate new slide creation based on existing slides, and import finished slides from other presentations. Finally, you'll print out your presentation, and run it (even on computers which don't have PowerPoint installed).

## Covers

# The PowerPoint screen

Below is a detailed illustration of the PowerPoint screen.

PowerPoint comes with an on-line magazine called 'PowerPoint Central'. This provides access to useful articles and tips; hyperlinks to Internet sites (clicking a link with your Internet connection open takes you to the site automatically); and (for CD users) links to a variety of extra features. To launch the magazine, pull down the Tools menu and click PowerPoint Central. Now follow the on-screen instructions.

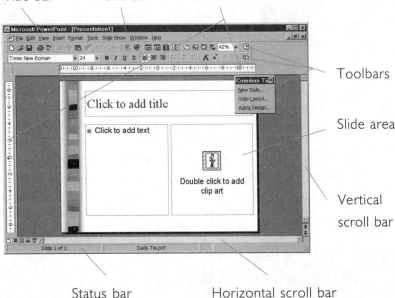

Title bar    Menu bar    Rulers

Toolbars

Slide area

Vertical scroll bar

Status bar    Horizontal scroll bar

Two of these components can be hidden, if required.

## Specifying which screen components display

Pull down the Tools menu and click Options. Then:

**1** Ensure the View tab is active

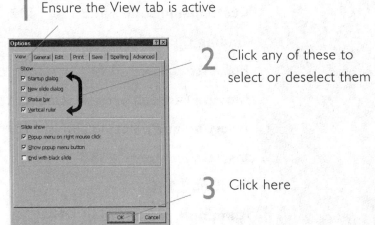

**2** Click any of these to select or deselect them

**3** Click here

# The AutoContent Wizard

**REMEMBER**

**You can also launch the Wizard when you start PowerPoint. Do the following:**

In Section 1, we looked at how to create new Office documents based on templates and Wizards. PowerPoint has a unique and particularly detailed Wizard which handles the basics of creating a presentation.

## Creating a new presentation with the AutoContent Wizard

Pull down the File menu and click New. Now do the following:

2 Click here

Click here

**Now follow the procedures on the right to complete the AutoContent Wizard dialogs.**

Ensure the Presentations tab is active

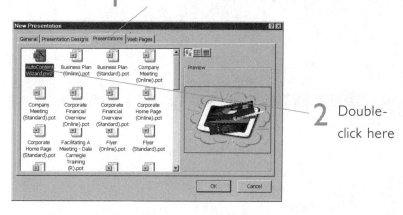

2 Double-click here

PowerPoint now launches the Wizard. Do the following:

**HANDY TIP**

**The Wizard produces a 'standard' slide show which you can amend later, if you want.**

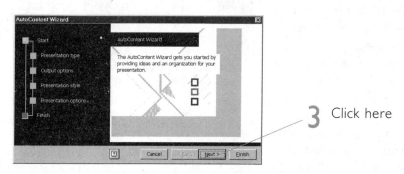

3 Click here

**REMEMBER**

**See Section 1 for how to create a blank presentation, or a slide show based on a template.**

Complete the remaining four dialogs in the normal way. In the final AutoContent dialog, click Finish to have PowerPoint generate the presentation.

# The slide views - an overview

PowerPoint has the following views:

*Slide*          displays each slide individually

*Outline*        shows the underlying textual structure of
                 the presentation

*Slide Sorter*   shows all the slides as icons, so you can
                 manipulate them more easily

*Notes Page*     shows each slide together with any
                 speaker's notes

These are different ways of looking at your presentation.
The best way to work with presentations is to use a
combination of all four, as appropriate.

## Switching to a view

Pull down the View menu and click Slide, Outline, Slide
Sorter or Notes Page.

The four views are shown below:

**The small window at the top right-hand corner of the Outline view is the Slide Miniature. It provides a 'thumbnail' view of the slide you're working on in Outline view, so that you know when you've entered too much text. (To hide the Miniature, pull down the View menu and deselect Slide Miniature).**

Slide View

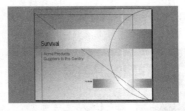

Outline View

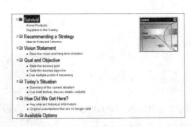

Slide Sorter View

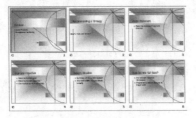

Notes Page View

# Using the slide views

The following are some brief supplemental notes on how best to use the PowerPoint views.

### Slide view

Slide view displays the current slide in its own window. Use Slide view when you want a detailed picture of a slide (for instance, when you amend any of the slide contents, or when you change the overall formatting).

To switch from slide to slide, you can press Page Up or Page Down as appropriate. For more information on how to move around in presentations, see 'Moving through presentations' later.

### Outline view

**All the views have their own default magnification. You can adjust this, however; simply pull down the View menu and click Zoom. In the Zoom dialog, type in a zoom % in the Percent field and click OK.**

If you're currently only working with the text in a given presentation, use Outline view. Outline view provides an overview of slide structure and content. The Slide Miniature – see page 130 – displays an accurate representation of the current slide for identification purposes.

### Slide Sorter view

If you need to rearrange the order of slides, use Slide Sorter view. You can simply click on a slide and drag it to a new location (to move more than one slide, hold down one Shift key as you click on them, then drag). You can also copy a slide by holding down Ctrl instead of Shift as you drag.

### Notes Page view

This view is an aid to the presenter rather than the viewer of the slide show. If you want to enter speaker's notes on a slide (for later printing), use Notes Page view.

In Notes Page view, the slide is displayed at a reduced size at the top of the page. Below this is a standard PowerPoint text object. For how to enter notes in this, see the 'Adding text to slides' topic later.

# Customising slide structure

The easiest way to customise the basic format of a slide is to use AutoLayout. AutoLayout offers a selection of 24 layout structures and lets you apply your choice to a specific slide or group of slides. When you've done this, you can then amend the individual components (see later topics).

### Using AutoLayout

**HANDY TIP**

**You can select more than one slide in Slide Sorter view by holding down one Shift key as you click on the slide icons.**

Make sure you're in Slide or Slide Sorter view. If you're in Slide Sorter view, click the slide(s) you want to amend. Pull down the Format menu and click Slide Layout. Then do the following:

Click a slide format

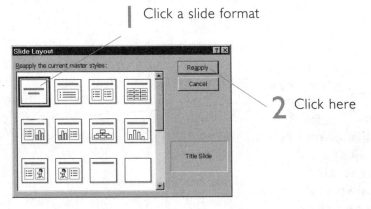

2 Click here

Any slide components present before you applied the new format will still remain. However, they may need to be resized or moved. Look at the illustration below:

**HANDY TIP**

**Standard mouse techniques can be used to reposition or rescale text objects in PowerPoint.**

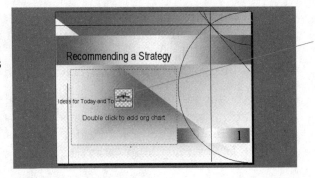

The imposition of the new format has meant that this text is now in the wrong location

# Adding text to slides

**To create a blank slide show, click New in the File menu. Click the General tab in the New Presentation dialog. Now double-click the Blank Presentation icon. Or, to create a blank slide show when you start PowerPoint, click Blank presentation in the launch dialog. Click OK.**

When you create a new slide show (unless you choose to create a blank presentation), PowerPoint fills each slide with placeholders containing sample text. The idea is that you should replace this with your own text.

The illustration below shows a sample slide before customisation:

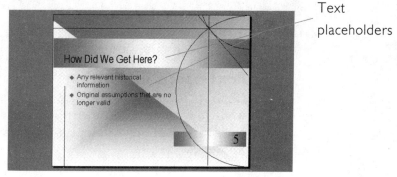

Text placeholders

**You can summarise specific slides. When you do this, PowerPoint collects the slide titles and inserts them into a new slide. In Slide Sorter view, select the relevant slides. Then click the Summary Slide button:**

**in the Slide Sorter toolbar. PowerPoint inserts the new slide in front of the first selected slide.**

To insert your own text, click in any text placeholder. PowerPoint displays a text entry box. Now do the following:

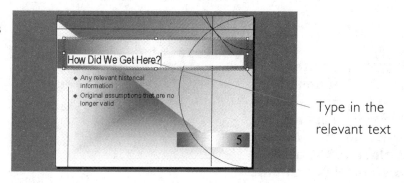

Type in the relevant text

Finally, click anywhere outside the placeholder to confirm the addition of the new text.

# Formatting text (1)

You can carry out a variety of formatting enhancements on text. You can:

- change the font and/or type size

- apply a font style or effect

- apply a colour

- specify the alignment

- specify the line spacing

### Font-based formatting

Click inside the relevant text object and select the text you want to format. Pull down the Format menu and click Font. Now carry out any of steps 1-6 below, as appropriate. Then follow step 7:

1 Click a new typeface

2 Type in a new point size

7 Click here

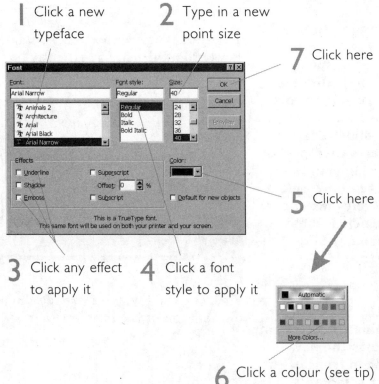

5 Click here

3 Click any effect to apply it

4 Click a font style to apply it

6 Click a colour (see tip)

**HANDY TIP**

**Re step 6 – if none of the colours here are suitable, click More Colors. In the new dialog, click a colour in the polygon in the centre. Then click OK. Follow step 7 to apply the new colour.**

# Formatting text (2)

### Changing text spacing

First, click inside the relevant text object and select the text whose spacing you want to amend. Pull down the Format menu and click Line Spacing. Now carry out any of steps 1-3 below, as appropriate. Then follow step 4.

Type in a line spacing

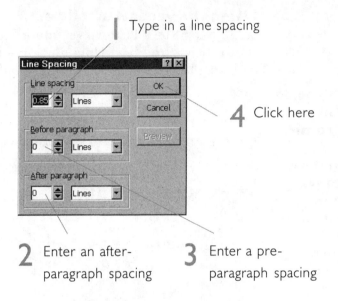

4 Click here

2 Enter an after-paragraph spacing

3 Enter a pre-paragraph spacing

### Changing text alignment

First, click inside the relevant text object and select the text whose alignment you want to amend. Pull down the Format menu and do the following:

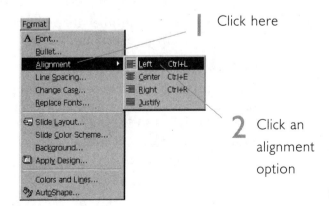

1 Click here

2 Click an alignment option

# Moving through presentations

Since presentations – by their very nature – always have more than one slide, it's essential to be able to move from slide to slide easily (it's even more essential in the case of especially large presentations). There are two main methods you can use to do this.

### Using the vertical scroll bar

In Slide or Notes Page views, move the mouse pointer over the vertical scroll box. Hold down the left mouse button and drag the box up or down. As you do so, PowerPoint displays a message box giving you the number and title of the slide you're up to.

**Of course, you can also click the vertical scroll bar arrows to move through your presentation in the normal way. However, the page number message doesn't then display.**

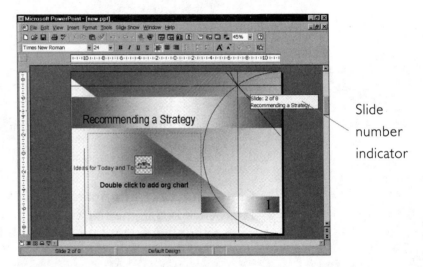

Slide number indicator

When the correct number displays, release the mouse button to jump to that slide.

### Using Slide Sorter view

Slide Sorter view offers a useful shortcut which you can use to jump immediately to a specific slide. Simply double-click any slide icon within Slide Sorter view; PowerPoint then switches to Slide view and displays the slide you selected.

# Inserting and deleting slides

**You can easily include existing slides from another slide show. Pull down the Insert menu and click Slides from Files. In the File field, type in the location of the second slide show; click Display. In the Select Slides section, click the slides you want to include:**

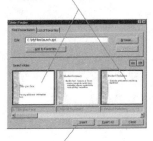

**Click Insert.**

**When you delete a slide, PowerPoint does not provide a message requiring your confirmation. The slide and its contents are erased immediately.**

You'll often want to insert a slide within the body of a presentation. There are also occasions when you'll need to delete a slide because it's no longer required. PowerPoint lets you do both easily and conveniently.

### Inserting a slide

In Slide view or Notes Page view, move to the slide that you want to precede the new one. In Outline view, click the icon – e.g. ⊠ – for the slide that you want to precede the new one. In Slide Sorter view, click the relevant slide. Then pull down the Insert menu and click New Slide.

Now do the following:

The current slide format is highlighted; click another if you want to apply a new format

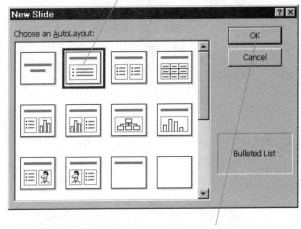

2 Click here

### Deleting a slide

In Slide view or Notes Page view, move to the slide that you want to delete. In Outline view, click the slide icon: ⊠ . In Slide Sorter view, click a slide (or hold down one Shift key as you click on multiple slide icons to delete more than one slide). Then pull down the Edit menu and click Delete Slide.

# Inserting pictures (1)

Click here

Pictures can help enormously in making your presentations visually effective. You can add pictures in two basic ways.

## Adding clip art

If the Office Clip Art Gallery is installed on your computer, you can do the following. Go to the slide into which you want the clip art added. Pull down the Insert menu and click Clip Art. Now carry out the following steps:

Activate the Clip Art tab

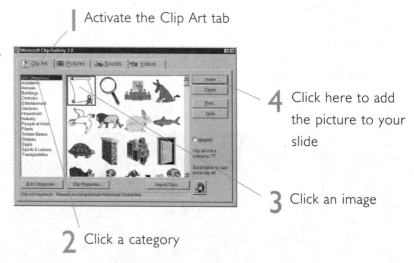

4 Click here to add the picture to your slide

3 Click an image

2 Click a category

A slide with an added clip-art image:

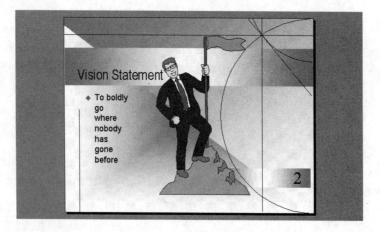

# Inserting pictures (2)

**HANDY TIP**

**Once inserted into a slide,** pictures can be resized and moved in the normal way.

Third-party images can be very useful in slides. They can be:

- output from other programs (e.g. drawings and illustrations)

- commercial clip art

- photographs

PowerPoint will happily translate a wide variety of third-party graphics formats.

### Adding a third-party picture

**HANDY TIP**

**To have a picture appear on every slide, insert it into the slide master (a template which applies to the overall slide show). Pull down the View menu and click Master, Slide Master. Now follow steps 1-4. To return to the active slide, do the following:**

To insert a picture produced by another program, do the following. In Slide view, go to the slide into which you want the clip art added. Pull down the Insert menu and click Picture, From File. Now carry out the following steps:

2 Click here. In the drop-down list, click the drive/folder that hosts the picture

4 Click here

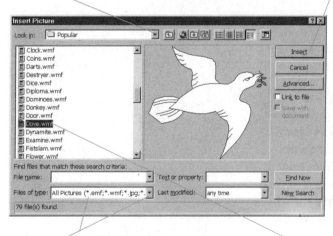

Click here

| Make sure All Pictures is shown. If it isn't, click the arrow and select it from the drop-down list

3 Click the picture file

# Printing

You can print any presentation component. These include:

- slides

- notes

- outlines

PowerPoint makes printing easy.

## Printing a presentation

Pull down the File menu and click Print. Now carry out any of steps 1-5 below, as appropriate. Finally, follow step 6.

1 Click here; select the printer you want from the list

2 Click here to print the current slide only

3 Type in the number of copies required

6 Click here

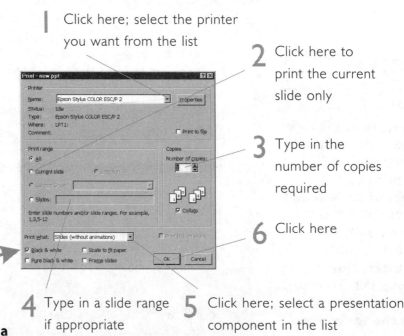

**Deselect Black & White if you have a colour printer and want to print out in colour.**

4 Type in a slide range if appropriate

5 Click here; select a presentation component in the list

## Fast-track printing

To print using all the default settings, without launching the Print dialog, simply click the Print button on the Standard toolbar:

# Running a presentation (1)

Once you've created (and possibly printed) your slide show, it's time to run it. Before you do so, however, you should set the run parameters.

When you run your presentation you can, if you want, have PowerPoint wait for your command before moving from slide to slide. This is useful if you anticipate being interrupted during the presentation. You retain full control over delivery.

Alternatively, you can have the slide show run automatically. Before you can do this, though, you have to set various parameters. These include the intervals between slides, which slides you want to run and the presentation type.

### Preparing to run your slide show

First, open the presentation you want to run. Then pull down the Slide Show menu and click Set Up Show. Now do the following:

**HANDY TIP**

**You can choose from a wide variety of presentation types. The first option – presentation by a speaker – is the most common.**

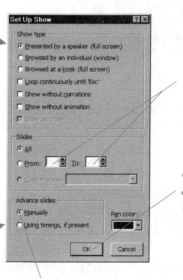

If you don't want all slides to run, enter start and end slide numbers

**3** Click here

**HANDY TIP**

**Re step 2 – click Using timings, if present to have the presentation run automatically.**

**2** Ensure this is selected if you want to control the slide show progression manually

# Running a presentation (2)

**If you want to jump directly to a specific slide, type the number and press Return.**

## Running a manual presentation

Pull down the Slide Show menu and click View Show. If you selected Manually in step 2 on page 141, PowerPoint runs the first slide of your presentation and pauses. When you're ready to move on to the next slide, left-click once or press Page Down. If you need to go back to the previous slide, simply press Page Up.

## Rehearsing an automatic presentation

Before you can run an automatic presentation, you have to set the slide intervals. You can do this by 'rehearsing' the slide show. Pull down the Slide Show menu and click Rehearse Timings, then do the following:

**You can also run your slide show on another computer (even one on which PowerPoint hasn't been installed). Pull down the File menu and click Pack and Go – this launches the Pack and Go Wizard. Follow the on-screen instructions.**

This timer counts the interval until the next slide; when the timing is right, follow step 2

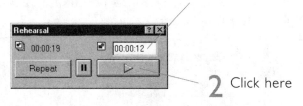

2 Click here

After step 2, PowerPoint moves to the next slide. Repeat steps 1 and 2 until all the slides have had intervals allocated. Finally, another message appears:

Click here

**If you want to end your slide show at any time, simply press Esc. This applies to manual and automatic presentations.**

## Running an automatic presentation

After rehearsal, pull down the Slide Show menu and click View Show. If you clicked Using timings, if present in step 2 on page 141, PowerPoint displays the first slide and moves on to subsequent slides after the rehearsed intervals have elapsed.

# Outlook

This chapter provides a brief introduction to the *stand-alone* (i.e. non-workgroup) use of Outlook. Use it to learn how to use the Outlook bar to launch any of Outlook's associated folders. You'll enter appointments/events, tasks and contact details; Outlook will then coordinate them so that you can manage your business/personal affairs more easily. You'll also set up and use Outlook to transmit and receive e-mail, using – if you want – Word 97 as your editor.

## Covers

**Section Five**

# The Outlook screen

Below is a detailed illustration of a typical Outlook screen.

**REMEMBER**

The Folder banner tells you which Outlook folder (in this case, Inbox – see page 145) is active.

Title bar          Menu bar          Toolbar

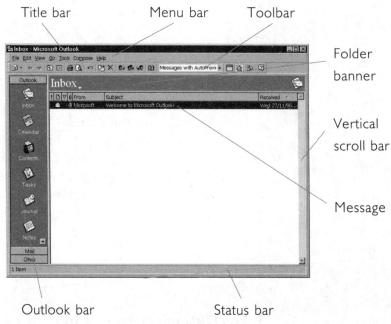

Folder banner

Vertical scroll bar

Message

Outlook bar                    Status bar

**HANDY TIP**

To print out work you do in any component on the Outlook bar, first click the relevant folder. Press Ctrl+P. Complete the Print dialog as normal. In particular, select a print style (the choices vary with the folder selected). (For more information on completing the Print dialog, see the relevant topic in earlier sections in this book). Finally, click OK to begin printing.

Some of these – e.g. the menu and scroll bars – are standard to just about all programs that run under Windows. However, you can specify which of the two available toolbars display.

## Specifying which toolbars display

Pull down the View menu and do the following:

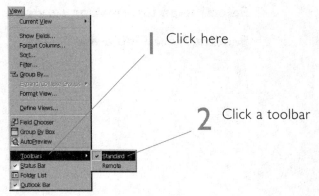

Click here

1

Click a toolbar

2

# Using the Outlook bar

**Outlook organises its features into folders. All folders are accessible from the Outlook bar.**

When you run Outlook, it automatically opens the Inbox. This is the Outlook folder in which incoming messages are stored. However, there are several additional folders you can access. These include:

| | |
|---|---|
| *Calendar* | A tool to help you schedule events, tasks, appointments and meetings |
| *Contacts* | A tool to help you manage business/personal contacts |
| *Tasks* | A task management aid |
| *Notes* | Acts as a jotting pad; you can create 'sticky' notes |
| *Mail* | Includes Inbox, and also these folders: |

— Sent Items

— Outbox

— Deleted items

**To insert a note, click the Notes folder in the Outlook bar. Press Ctrl+N. Do the following:**

Type in your note, then press Alt+F4

## Activating folders

Do the following:

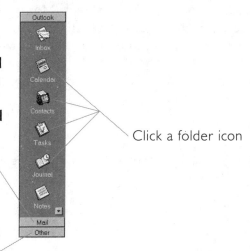

Click a folder icon

**Click Mail for access to additional delivery-based features.**

**Click Other for access to standard folders, e.g. My Computer.**

# Working with the Calendar (1)

**Outlook has another folder which you can use to oversee your schedule: Journal. You can have Journal record messages, meetings and task requests automatically. It will also record Office documents.**

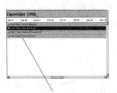

Auto-recorded entries

**To specify what is recorded in Journal, click the Journal icon in the Outlook bar. Click Options in the Tools menu. In the Journal tab, make the relevant selections. Click OK.**

**See page 144 for how to make the Standard toolbar visible.**

The Calendar provides alternative ways of viewing and interacting with your schedules. The main views are:

*Day/Week/Month*

The all-purpose view. An aspect of the Appointment Book; used to enter appointments, events and tasks. You can specify whether you work in the Day, Week or Month aspects. (See below.)

*Active Appointments*

An aspect of the Appointment Book; used to enter and monitor active appointments.

*Events*

An aspect of the Appointment Book, useful for entering and monitoring events.

Some aspects of Outlook – for instance, the use of the Calendar to coordinate meetings among workgroup members – are beyond the scope of this book.

## Switching between the Day, Week and Month Calendars

You'll probably use Day/Week/Month view more than any other, because it offers great flexibility. By default, the Calendar displays appointments etc. with the use of the Day aspect. To change the aspect, refer to the Standard toolbar and click any of the following:

Week format

Day/Week/Month

Day format          Month format

# Working with the Calendar (2)

You can add appointments to the Daily Calendar.

If you want, you can stipulate that the appointment is recurring (i.e. it's automatically entered at an interval you specify).

**HANDY TIP** **Re step 2 -
if the date
shown in
the Date
Navigator isn't
correct, click the
following:**
◀ **or** ▶
**to go back or
forward by one
month respectively.**

## Adding an appointment in the Daily Calendar

Carry out steps 1, 2 and 3 below (then follow the procedures in the Remember tip if you want to mark the appointment as recurring):

2 Click the correct day

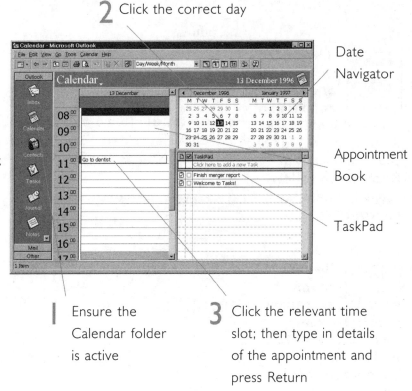

Date Navigator

Appointment Book

TaskPad

**REMEMBER** **To mark an
appointment
as
recurring,
carry out steps 1-3.
Then double-click
the appointment. In
the toolbar within
the dialog which
launches, click this
button:**

**In the Appointment
Recurrence dialog,
set the relevant
options. Click OK.
Now click the
following:**

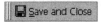

1 Ensure the Calendar folder is active

3 Click the relevant time slot; then type in details of the appointment and press Return

Outlook adds the new appointment to the Calendar.

# Working with the Calendar (3)

You can add events to the Daily Calendar.

Outlook handles events in a rather different way to appointments. For example, they don't occupy specific time slots in your Appointment Book. Instead, they can relate to any day and can even extend over more than one.

Outlook distinguishes between events and annual events. Annual events occur yearly on a specific date.

Examples of events include:

**If you need to amend or update an existing event, double-click its button within the Appointment Book. Then follow steps 1-3 here, as appropriate.**

- birthdays and anniversaries

- shows

- seminars

Events display as buttons within the Appointment Book.

## Adding an event to the Daily Calendar

Right-click the relevant date/time slot. In the menu, click New Event. Now do the following:

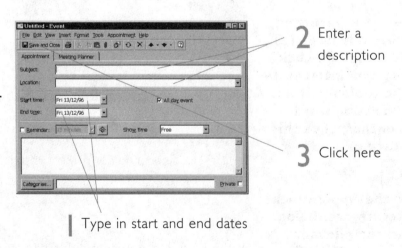

2 Enter a description

3 Click here

Type in start and end dates

**Re step 1 – to insert an *annual* event, instead of a start and end date, simply type in the date on which you want the annual event to recur.**

To mark an event as recurring, carry out steps 1-3 above. Then double-click the event in the Appointment Book. Now follow the procedures set out in the Remember tip on page 147.

# Working with the Calendar (4)

Use the Weekly view as an alternative way to display your appointments and events.

In the Weekly Calendar, you can enter appointments and events in the same way that you can in the Daily Calendar – see 'Working with the Calendar (1)' and 'Working with the Calendar (2)' for how to do this.

### Moving around in the Weekly Calendar

You can jump to a specific date in the Weekly Calendar. To do this, pull down the Go menu and click Go to Date. Carry out steps 1-4 and 7:

 **You can also use the Go To Date dialog (from within any Calendar view) to switch between the Day, Week and Month Calendars. Follow steps 5-7.**

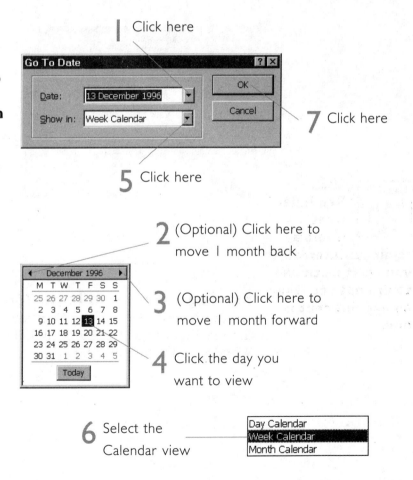

1 Click here

7 Click here

5 Click here

2 (Optional) Click here to move 1 month back

3 (Optional) Click here to move 1 month forward

4 Click the day you want to view

6 Select the Calendar view

# Working with the Calendar (5)

Use the Monthly Calendar to gain a useful overview of your schedule.

It's not a good idea, however, to use it to insert appointments directly; you can do so, but you may well find that the scale is too small to make the process convenient. Instead, use the following method.

### Inserting a new appointment in the Monthly Calendar

Right click in the Calendar. In the menu which launches, click New Appointment. Then carry out steps 1-3 below:

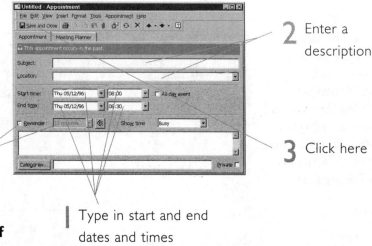

2 Enter a description

3 Click here

1 Type in start and end dates and times

**HANDY TIP**
**Click Reminder (then insert a reminder interval) if you want Outlook to prompt you when an appointment is due.**

### Inserting a new event in the Monthly Calendar

You can insert events in the Monthly Calendar by using the same techniques as for the Daily Calendar. See the 'Working with the Calendar (3)' topic earlier.

# Working with the Tasks folder

Use the Tasks folder to enter and track tasks.

When you've entered a task into the Tasks folder, it displays in the TaskPad in the Daily and Weekly Calendars.

### Entering a task

If the Tasks folder isn't already active, click the Tasks icon in the Outlook bar. Then do the following:

 **If you need to amend or update an existing task, click within it and follow steps 1 and 2.**

2 Type in a due date

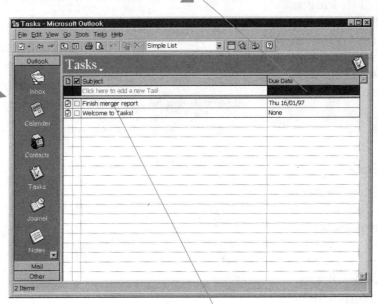

 **Various views are available in the Tasks folder. To switch between views, click Current View in the View menu; select a view in the sub-menu.**

Click here in a new row; type in a task description

 **Tasks can be prioritised. Outlook recognises three levels: Low, Normal and High.**

### Customising tasks

The above steps produce a basic task. If you want to customise the settings in more depth (for instance, you can set start and end dates, reminder intervals and/or priority levels), double-click the task. Complete the dialog which launches, then click Save and Close.

# Working with the Contacts folder

**Another view – Detailed Address Cards – uses the card model but with even more detail...**

**To switch between views, click Current View in the View menu; select a view in the sub-menu.**

**If you need to amend a contact, double-click it. Then carry out steps 3-4 as appropriate.**

**To set advanced contact details, click any of the tabs here: Complete the relevant fields then carry out step 4.**

Use the Contacts folder as a convenient place to keep track of business/personal contacts.

Outlook displays contacts in various forms. The two main ones are:

- as a grid

- using a business card model

You can enter contacts directly into either, but you may find that the business card view makes the job easier.

## Entering a contact

If the Contacts view isn't already active, click the Contacts icon in the Outlook bar. Then do the following:

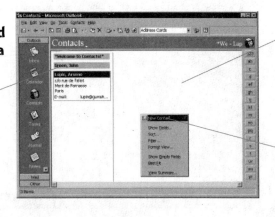

1 Right-click anywhere here

2 Click here

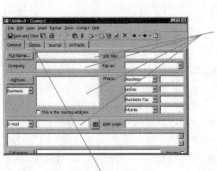

3 Enter contact details

4 Click here

# Selecting an information service

**A user profile consists of settings which define how Outlook operates. It determines (among other things) how Outlook sends and receives mail via one or more associated information services.**

You can use Outlook to send and receive e-mail. Before you can do this, however, you need to:

• install an information service

• add it to your user profile

Several information services (e.g. Internet Mail) are automatically installed with Outlook.

## Adding an information service

Pull down the Tools menu and click Services. Now do the following:

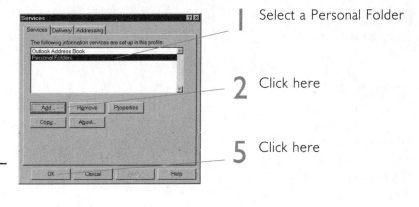

I   Select a Personal Folder

2   Click here

5   Click here

**Re step 3 – if none of the installed information services is suitable, click Have Disk. Insert the necessary disk, complete the Install Other Information Service dialog and then click OK. Follow the on-screen instructions.**

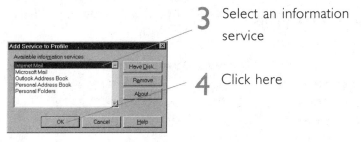

3   Select an information service

4   Click here

Outlook now launches further dialogs, according to which information service was selected. Complete these as appropriate. Then carry out step 5 above. Finally, close and restart Outlook, then refer to page 154.

# Sending/receiving e-mail

REMEMBER

**Mail which you've written but which hasn't yet been sent is lodged in the Outbox folder. Mail which *has* been despatched is lodged in the Sent Items folder. To access either folder, click:**

| Mail |

**in the Outlook bar.**

If you followed the procedures on page 153, you'll now be in a position to send and receive e-mail via Outlook. (Unless you specified otherwise, Outlook establishes your Internet connection automatically on startup.)

## Sending e-mail

If the Inbox isn't currently open, click the Inbox icon in the Outlook bar. Pull down the Compose menu and click New Mail Message. Do the following:

Complete these sections

2 Click here

## Receiving e-mail

HANDY TIP

**Re step 1 – for help with addressing the e-mail, click the To button. In the Select Names dialog, double-click the correct recipient name. Click OK.**

To view received e-mail messages, click the Inbox folder in the Outlook bar. Now double-click any message entry. Do the following:

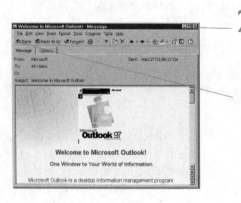

2 Click here to close the original message

REMEMBER

**You can use Word to write your e-mail. Click Options in the Tools menu. In the E-mail tab, select Use Word as the e-mail editor. Click OK.**

1 Click here if you want to reply to the message. Outlook opens another Message window; enter your response and click Send.

# Index